Public Assembly Facilities

Public Assembly Facilities
Planning and Management

DON JEWELL
Event and Facility Consultant

A Wiley-Interscience Publication
John Wiley & Sons
New York   Chichester   Brisbane   Toronto

Library of Congress Cataloging in Publication Data

Jewell, Don, 1921-
   Public assembly facilities.

  "A Wiley-Interscience publication."
  Includes index.
    1. Auditoriums.   2. Theaters.   3. Stadia.
4. Convention facilities.   5. Exhibition buildings.

  I. Title.

NA6815.J45   725'.8   77-16524
ISBN 0-471-02437-6

To the International Association of Auditorium Managers and its membership, for more than 50 years of untiring effort to improve and professionalize management practices.

Preface

If cities as we know them today are to survive, then we must provide the things that make us civilized—theater, sports, culture.

These words by Alan Cohen, president of Madison Square Garden, at the dedication of Yankee Stadium in New York, could have been expressed at the opening of almost every public assembly facility throughout the years.

Communities evidently reflect the attitude of Mr. Cohen when it is realized that audience support structures in North America alone represent an investment of billions in public and private dollars. Development of new accommodations for conventions, performing arts, and sports can be expected to continue in the years ahead.

The industry, however, must be considered as singular in nature with only a few of the larger cities boasting of more than one major stadium or one arena or music hall. Rare is the architect who has had the opportunity to build more than one such facility during his career. Most suppliers find they cannot survive solely on the business generated by audience support facilities.

Presented as a guide and resource for architects and planners, governmental agencies, public officials, administrators, and others interested in facility construction and management, the following pages contain a wide variety of information on arenas, stadiums, theaters, convention centers, and exhibition halls.

The subject matter represents the collective views and opinions of many facility managers, expressed in conversations, articles prepared for various publications, and papers delivered in management seminars. Some of the statements have been repeated and rewritten by so many in so many ways that their origin is, in many cases, no longer traceable.

The concepts come also after many years of personal operating experience and visits to hundreds of public assembly buildings throughout the United States, Canada, Mexico, and Europe.

No attempt is intended to suggest specific solutions to architectural problems of designing a public assembly facility. Quantification and detail can be developed only in response to the individual requirements of a particular project. Rather it is hoped that the generalized subjects discussed will serve to alert facility planners to some of the considerations that must be resolved.

Perhaps unique in this day of advance education, public assembly facility management remains one of those for which no particular formal training is available at any recognized university or college. An annual week-long symposium for managers is currently offered by the University of Illinois in conjunction with the International Association of Auditorium Managers, but beyond that the only training is "on the job." Indeed, a survey today would probably reveal that most active managers assumed their initial facility management assignment with no previous experience in the field.

It is hoped that this book will become a primary source of reference material for study by all those seriously interested in the planning and management of public assembly facilities. It should also prove helpful in acquainting newly appointed board members and other administrators with a somewhat basic overview of the industry.

DON JEWELL

Portland, Oregon
October 1977

Contents

Public Assembly Facilities

Introduction

If the contention that entertainment in one form or another is almost as old as humanity itself, it must surely follow that public assembly facilities cannot have been far behind.

Writing in *A Pictorial History of the American Circus,* John and Alice Durant point out that Sir Arthur Evans, excavator of Knossus on the Island of Crete, proved that circuslike acts were witnessed by audiences some 2400 years before Christ. Sir Arthur's claim is supported by a wall painting of what was then known as "bull leaping." This ancient stunt was performed by trained Cretan youths and staged circus-fashion in an arena before onlookers who sat in elevated seats.

Perhaps one of the best known of the very early facilities was Rome's Circus Maximus, an enormous structure, 625-yd long, with seats for more than 150,000 persons. Completed in 329 B.C., it served primarily as a course for chariot races but was often the scene of wholesale slaughter.

A later development was another kind of Roman arena, the amphitheater. Smaller than the circus and bowlshaped, it gave spectators a closer view of the action. One of the largest was the Flavian Amphitheatre, now known as the Colosseum. Located in the southeast corner of the Forum between Palatine Hill and Esquiline Hill, this imposing Roman antiquity was begun in A.D. 72 by Vespian and finished in A.D. 80 by Titus of the Flavian family. Various sources give the seating capacity as 50,000 to 80,000 persons.

Meanwhile, on a higher cultural level the outdoor theater, devoted to drama, was developing in the Grecian world. On still another level the accommodation of large crowds for political and religious purposes was also becoming evident.

The gradual appearance of covered structures to protect the public from the elements followed as a logical evolution of need, population growth, and construction capabilities.

In America the colonial log cabin perhaps housed the first public gathering. This early meeting house served not only for regular assemblies but as a refuge in times of danger or emergency, and in this one building much of the life of the community was focused.

The meeting house of the seventeenth and eighteenth centuries thus became the forerunner of the town hall, opera house, theater, concert hall, or whatever name it may have been given. With both need and community pride as incentives, the nineteenth century saw the construction of hundreds of "town halls" throughout the land, most of which were designed to be all things to all people. Often constructed with a low stage, a flat floor and portable seating, this auditorium served as theater, lecture or concert hall, arena for athletic events, voting place on election day, and drill room for the National Guard.

In larger communities the town hall was followed by more sophisticated, single-purpose structures such as New York's Carnegie Hall. Elsewhere, and especially in smaller cities which lacked the funds to support single or even dual-purpose halls, came the generation of supposedly all-purpose facilities with such names as Municipal or City Auditorium.

Supported by the Public Works Administration (PWA), a flurry of public assembly facilities was built in the 1930s, some of which had two halls under a common roof. Some offered a single stage to be shared by concert hall and arena. Others contained exhibition space. In their attempt to serve everyone the "PWA buildings" failed in most part to perform any function well. Acoustics were poor, sightlines questionable, and support facilities grossly inadequate. These buildings were expensive to operate and most lost money.

The availability of facilities, however, did serve to create the need for more traveling attractions to fill their schedules. The arena maintained some of the all-purpose characteristics of the town hall—a place for sports, conventions, exhibits, dances, and banquets; in short, a good place for people to gather in large numbers of perhaps 5000 to 15,000. Ice shows became popular, rodeos and circuses moved indoors, and many events could at last be enjoyed in air-conditioned comfort.

The end of wartime austerity in the late 1940s brought an explosion of arena and stadium construction. In the fifties and sixties cities sought to outdo one another in providing facilities for professional baseball, football, basketball and hockey.

Moving with almost equal speed in the late fifties and sixties was the introduction of the ever larger and better appointed convention center or complex. Hungrily anticipating a share of the $4 billion meetings industry, community after community throughout North America envisioned an added means of developing a strong local economy.

The thrust resulted in giant-sized exhibition halls that contained hundreds of thousands of square feet of display space, and well-equipped assembly areas and meeting rooms. Most had complete kitchens, lounges, and other amenities for the comfort of convention or conference delegates.

But if big was good, bigger was better, and the domed stadiums of the 1970s made their appearance. From the Houston Astrodome, the first of its kind, to the Seattle Kingdome the story has been much the same. These giant facilities serve major sports such as football and baseball in a grand style that spares the spectators any concern for the rigors of weather.

New architectural concepts such as the use of cables and fabric to cover long spans can be expected to make an impact on almost all future structures for large audiences. Some architects and designers are forcefully stating that topless stadiums are already in the past.

On a smaller scale a popular newcomer to the public assembly facility field is the less expansive and more intimate conference center. Developed originally in resort-type settings, it is now being constructed in smaller communities to attract a specific, but highly desirable, segment of the conventions and meetings market.

FACILITIES MANAGEMENT

Serving as a cohesive mechanism throughout the last half-century for the exhange of information and development of management techniques in the field of public assembly facilities has been the International Association of Auditorium Managers. Established in December 1924 by six auditorium managers, the IAAM has grown in membership to more than 800 men and women who represent facilities valued at billions of dollars in publicly and privately invested funds.

These prime buildings and complexes offer the public in excess of 30 million square feet of exhibit space, more than six million permanent seating accommodations, and untold numbers of portable seats and bleachers; they also boast of more than 2500 multipurpose rooms with a capacity of 87,350 to 346,000 persons, depending on room arrangement, and attract millions of paid-admission patrons anually to every type of event imaginable.

By the efforts of IAAM, annual management symposiums, new managers' seminars, and other training programs are made available. The association provides a system of accreditation for members seeking the rank of "Certified Facilities Executive" and honors its leaders with the Charles A. McElravy Award for "outstanding contributions to the profession of auditorium management and service to the International Association of Auditorium Managers." Its computerized Industry Profile Survey has become a highly regarded source of the industry's data and practices.

1. Programming and Planning

To construct the public assembly facility most needed by a community is perhaps the best formula for a successful project, but deciding *what* to build often proves more difficult.

All too often projects are launched on the basis of personal desires, competition with other cities, community pride, political pressures, business influences, and a score of similar reasons. From such beginnings have come many of those buildings that will remain a tax burden on their cities for many years to come.

In some situations the need for a performing arts center or a convention hall may be obvious. In others, however, the first step in planning is to determine carefully what—if anything—is required.

Ideally, an investigation of a community's current demands should include an inventory of existing facilities, followed by an examination of future requirements. In most cases accommodations for sports, shows, exhibitions, conventions, concerts, and other cultural events may be included. Further study will fix seating capacities, floor dimensions, number of meeting rooms, and other specifics.

Feasibility studies of one kind or another are one of the normal beginning points for most communities interested in the development of new or expanded facilities. These studies may be directed toward a broad assessment of community requirements or sometimes toward determining the need for a hall to serve a specific purpose or segment of the community.

It is at this point that the marketability, or perhaps usability, of a building should be closely scrutinized. A city, state, county, or province rarely, if ever, erects a building or complex of this kind for its own use. *A governmental body customarily builds a facility for leasing to others.* If the potential user or lessee finds that he does not want it, that he cannot afford the rent, or that it fails to fill his requirements, the building may stand idle a great part of the time.

Even the greatest of designs and plans may be of little help if the structure does not meet its intended purpose.

Misconceptions or misinterpretations of industry practices, community requirements, the convention market, or other demands often constitute much of the problem. Greater attention to advance planning should result in facilities that not only serve their communities better but should also provide greater revenues and lower operating costs.

Perhaps the most difficult decisions for many community leaders to reach are those regarding size and seating capacities. The concept that "if big is good, bigger is better" may well result in a costly building that will fall far short of meeting what may be the modest requirements of potential users.

Conversely, to construct a facility incapable of meeting the demands of a growing area or activity would be equally inacceptable.

Many exceptions exist throughout the United States and Canada, but generally speaking a community cannot ignore its geographic location, transportation schedules, population, economy, or the interests of its residents. In other words, a traveling show must be able to reach a given city on a reasonable routing; a convention delegate must travel on an acceptable itinerary; enough people must reside in the area to support attractions financially, and finally there must be an appreciation and understanding on the part of the citizens of the presentations offered.

The goal, it would seem, would be a facility "tailor-made" for its community, but at the same time recognizing the specific or peculiar needs of that building's users or lessees.

From a functional standpoint the floor plan of the building must reflect the affinity of certain activities for one another; for example, box office or admission control offices and functions should have direct access to the lobby or "front-of-the-house" areas, dressing rooms must be near the playing floor or stage, and meeting rooms must relate to the exhibition area.

Operationally, the relation of one function to another is equally important. The design of the seating form may well dictate the employment of additional ushers or usherettes for the life of the building. Inadequate attention to a functional trash disposal system may add thousands of dollars in custodial workers wages. Improper location or sizing of concessions stands and their support areas may well contribute to a continuing loss of sales and/or net profits, lack of an efficient system of disposing of rink ice may result in the loss of potential rental days, and so on.

A leading architectural publication once reported that a nationally recognized firm built its structures on "talk, talk, endless communal talk." Such communication of information can help all parties concerned to reach a thorough understanding of the facility and its function before the plans are drawn.

Experience indicates that the group or "team" approach is resulting in steady improvements in facilities of all types. Included should be:

- A thorough study of the feasibility, viability, or desirability of a given facility or complex.
- Selection of a competent architect as well as qualified consultants in specialized areas.
- Employment of an *experienced* manager or consultant to assist the architect in operational and functional matters and to aid the "owner" in reaching those decisions for which he will be responsible.

Construction of a building for public assembly may often be a major undertaking for a given public body or governmental agency. Greater sums of money are being spent; therefore the results will be viewed more closely and the facility used more by the public than almost any other community project.

In a majority of instances local architects will be engaged to design and plan the buildings. For most it may be their one—and sometimes only——opportunity of this kind. As a tribute to the profession and its members, most buildings reflect good design and dedicated research on the part of their architects. The architect is handicapped, however, if he is denied a budget large enough to provide for the employment of professional assistance or consultation in many of the highly specialized areas such as admissions control, concessions, catering, and acoustics.

Not only may the architect be embarked on *his* only public assembly facility assignment but the same may be true of the public owners. As the architect turns to the "owner" for decisions, it is here that a consultant can be of the greatest assistance in providing the performance requirements and alternatives that must be considered in order to reach proper conclusions.

General concensus once favored retention of a manager or director to serve as the professional representative at the earliest stages of the project. Although appealing in concept, the practical experience of many communities has shown that few managers available for new facilities can bring to the project the degree of experience necessary to provide correct responses to the architect. More often than not the long process of planning and construction takes its toll in one form or another and results in an unfortunately high rate of managerial "fatalities."

Seldom does an authority find itself in a position to engage the services of a manager with experience in more than one or two facilities. Rarely is one who has planning or construction expertise to be found. Often, although well meaning, this individual brings to his new assignments only the knowledge, and sometimes the prejudices, gained in his former employment. Through no fault of his own he has not had the exposure of working under a wide variety of conditions and circumstances.

More and more communities are discovering that it is more satisfactory and economical to engage the services of operational and management consultants to work closely with the architects, city officials, and prospective clients and then assist in the recruitment of a full-time manager or director at a reasonable time in advance of opening the building or complex. The manager's primary concerns can then be proper staffing, establishment of administrative offices, and scheduling of events.

Such a process would result in substantial savings to a community by eliminating the on-going salary plus fringe benefits and also permit a delay in the selection of a manager until the time that objectives, policies, and requirements of the facility were more clearly defined.

2. Semantics of the Industry

Few industries have encountered more difficulty in developing a uniform nomenclature for its buildings, job titles, and associated activities than has the construction and management of public assembly facilities. It is, in fact, a profession that so far has been unable to develop an adequate vocabulary.

Even the professional organization to which its managers belong is called the International Association of Auditorium Managers. Still, only a small percentage of its membership actually manage auditoriums. Most are responsible for sports arenas, convention centers, music halls, stadiums or exhibition halls.

In the mid-1960s "public assembly facility" began to gain in favor as an all-encompassing term. In 1966 it was used in the title of an IAAM publication, "Planning and Management of Public Assembly Facilities."

9

The IAAM now offers certification for its managers by granting to those qualified the designation of "Certified Facilities Executive."

One of the early attempts to classify facilities was undertaken by T. J. Millisack, manager of general services for the City and County of Denver, in an article for *The American City* entitled, "Are You Planning a Municipal Auditorium?"

Theater. A theater unit normally should contain between 1,200 and 1,600 fixed seats, regardless of the size of the community. A smaller theater cannot be operated economically if the city expects to lease the theater for "road" shows. A theater larger than this capacity sacrifices the "intimate" and acoustical qualities essential to successful stage shows. The width of the proscenium of such a unit should be approximately 36 feet. Other features are usually keyed to these size factors.

Concert Hall. The size and seating capacity of a concert hall should be ideally limited to a maximum of 3,000 seats, regardless of the size of the community. It may be smaller, but if much smaller it can be combined with the theater. The proscenium arch of a concert hall should be about 55 feet in width. Most other features of the concert hall are keyed to these size factors.

Arena. The size of an arena should be scaled to the size of the community and in proportion to the size of the concert hall. In a broad sense, it should have a fixed seating capacity that is at least double that of the concert hall. The maximum seating capacity of the arena is more difficult to pinpoint. There is often a tendency to scale the minimum size of the arena to a single event that may be traditional. (April 1955, pp. 108–110.)

The International City Managers' Association has also wrestled with proper identification making one of its first attempts to classify buildings in 1959. The criteria were established by William E. Besuden, writing in "Planning and Management of Municipal Auditoriums," Report 185, *Management Information Service,* International City Managers Association, Chicago. (one of a series of reports available only to subscribers to the service). Besuden classified facilities as follows:

1. Arena. A large open floor area designed primarily to serve athletic events.
2. Exhibition Hall. A large open floor area to provide display space for large convention exhibits and trade shows; may include special equipment for booths, lighting, storage and loading and unloading of display items.
3. Music Hall. A large area with permanent seating for concerts and similar events; usually has a wide, shallow stage and special acoustical design. (June 1959, p.1)

For purposes of surveys, industry identification, and similar uses some variation of the two descriptive outlines would appear close.

In 1966, in the IAAM publication *Planning and Management of Public Assembly Facilities,* the IAAM Publications Committee offered the following classifications:

1. Auditoriums, Theaters. Theater-type structure generally with fixed seating and a stage. Seating ranges from a few hundred or less to 5,000 and in some cases more than this latter figure.
2. Coliseums, Arenas. Buildings with large seating capacities grouped around an open center area or arena. Most of the seats are fixed, although temporary seating can usually be added to enlarge the capacity. These range in size from those with a few hundred seats to those with a capacity in the neighborhood of 20,000.
3. Exhibition Halls. Flat floor structures of various sizes with no fixed or permanent seating capacity. These are used for public or trade exhibitions where manufacturers, dealers and others display their wares to potential buyers.

Actual names of these facilities pose even greater problems of identification. Classic examples are the "Memorial Coliseum" in Los Angeles, an outdoor stadium designed for football and seating about 92,600 persons, and the "Memorial Coliseum" in Fort Wayne, Indiana, an indoor arena built for basketball and hockey and seating about 10,000 persons.

For those who would plan and design "audience-support facilities" (a term coined by John Sherwood of Hammer, Siler, George Associates) some of the terminologies, definitions, and identifications currently in use are listed.

Personnel identifications that may be unique to the industry include the following:

Association executive   Usually the head (executive director, executive vice president, etc.) of an organization in a management capacity. He may also serve as the convention manager in smaller associations and may or may not serve as exhibit or show manager. He is often referred to as a "meetings planner."

Decorator   The decorator and his company normally work under contract or agreement with an association or show management to set up booths, drape walls, and perform similar tasks. As "official decorator" he has the opportunity to rent carpeting and other booth equipment, such as tables and chairs, to the show's exhibitors.

Drayage contractor   Most large exhibitions have an official drayage contractor. All exhibit displays and merchandise are consigned to this drayage firm. On arrival in a city the shipments are placed in storage until the agreed day of ingress into the exhibition hall. It is the responsibility of the drayage contractor to deliver exhibit merchandise to the correct booth and later remove the empty crates. At the close of the show he returns the crates and/or boxes to the booths and then assists exhibitors in shipping their displays to the next show, back to the factory, or to some other destination.

Event supervisor   This individual has the responsibility of representing the facility during the term of the event. The lessee is instructed to call on the event supervisor for additional equipment, emergency maintenance, or other types of service.

Houseman   A term perhaps more common in the hotel industry, a house-man or utility person is one whose primary responsibility is setting up tables and chairs for meetings, food service, and other purposes. They are normally assigned to service the room during meetings and later to perform take-down and cleaning duties.

Lessee   The licensee, lessee, or permittee is the individual or company that has leased the facility or a portion of it for a given event or function.

Promoter   Sometimes called the presenter or entrepreneur, the promoter is the individual or firm that has contracted with an act or event for a specific date or dates and has then leased an audience support facility in which to present the show. He is also responsible for all advertising and promotion. If income exceeds expenses, the profit will be his.

Stage carpenter   As the name implies, the stage carpenter is a stagehand but is primarily charged with responsibilities that call for construction or building skills.

Stage electrician   The electrician is also a stagehand, but his first respon-sibilities are the show's lighting and electrical requirements. In exhibit shows the "official electrician" is responsible for providing the distribution harness that supplies power to each booth. The harness is attached to the facility's energy sources. He is also permitted to rent special lighting and/or electrical equipment to the exhibitors.

Stagehand   A stagehand is a member of IATSE (International Alliance of Theater and Stage Employees). His responsibility is to perform the myriad services and tasks behind the scenes, which can range anywhere from raising and lowering curtains to handling scenery and properties.

Show manager   Sometimes called the exhibit manager, a show manager is usually responsible for laying out and selling space for a convention trade show. He may also represent an association in its dealings with the hall management and decorator. In commercial or consumer shows the show manager may be the owner or promoter or he may represent the company presenting the attraction.

Wardrobe women or dressers   Wardrobe women or dressers are responsible for the care of costumes and assist actors and performers in their preparations for appearing on stage.

The following is a short glossary of a few of the more familiar stage or entertainment terms:

Acting area   The area of the stage visible to the audience and used by the actors after the curtain rises.

Apron   The area of the stage in front of the curtain extending to the edge of the orchestra pit.

Batten   A long strip of wood used at the top and bottom of a drop or for framing flats. A pipe batten is a length of pipe to which a set of lines in the rigging system is hooked or tied.

Continental seating   A seating arrangement not interrupted by a center aisle.

Counterweight system   A permanent installation by which arbors or carriages are guided by wires from the stage level or fly gallery to a loading platform.

Cyclorama   A C-shaped sky representation, hung without folds and requiring at least two sets of lines for hanging.

Fixed spots   Spot lights or floodlights that are focused and preset before a performance. They may be turned on and off but cannot be moved during the action.

Flats   Stage flats are elevated platforms or risers designed to fold flat when not in use.

Flies   The space below the gridiron and above the acting area, not within sight of the audience. Flown units hang in the flies.

Fly   A verb indicating the backstage venacular for raising scenery into the flies by means of lines.

Fly gallery   A backstage area containing the fly floor, the pinrail and the tie-off rail. Ideally, this region should be approximately 16 feet above the floor level, provided there is a high fly loft.

Fly loft   The place directly below the gridiron in which the scenery hangs.

Gels   The gellatin sheets that produce different colored show lighting. They are normally used in a frame over a fixed or follow spot.

Follow spots   High-intensity spotlights capable of being moved about to follow the movement of a performer or actor.

Gridiron   Sometimes called a "grid," the gridiron is the metal framework directly below the ceiling of the stage house to which sheaves are attached.

House seats   Seats normally reserved for house management, show management, members of the cast, or their special guests. They are not sold but are held for special use.

Leg   A vertical masking frame of drapes placed at the side of the acting area for masking and decorative purposes.

Lines   Manila (hemp) ropes arranged in groups of three or four to complete the rigging system and permit the raising and lowering of heavy objects.

Long line   The stage line that extends the farthest distance from the pinrail.

Loading platform or dock   A backstage location referring to the level at which counterweights are placed in the carriages. The term sometimes applies to the raised area directly outside the loading door of the stage.

Orchestra   An architectural term that refers to the main floor of the auditorium. The orchestra pit separates the stage from the orchestra. In concert halls the orchestra shell is the framework that surrounds the orchestra.

Paid count   This term usually represents the total number of tickets actually sold for a given performance. As opposed to the "gate count" or "total count" of all persons attending.

Pinrail   A rail at which the lines from the gridiron are tied off.

Proscenium arch   The opening in the wall that separates the stage from the seating area.

Revolving stage   A special type of stage floor that revolves around a central pivot.

Rigging   The entire system of ropes, loft blocks, head blocks, manila ropes, pipe battens, and belaying pins.

Scalping   The practice of buying tickets at the printed price and reselling them at a higher figure.

Scrim   An open-weave fabric of coarse twisted thread with square and oblong openings. Thin paint or dye can be applied and the material will remain translucent.

Sight lines   The lines of vision of the spectators seated in normal and extreme positions in the facility. Sight lines include upper as well as side views.

Stage house   The entire backstage area from the floor to the ceiling.

Stage left   That portion of the acting area to the performer's left—the audiences' right.

Stage right   That portion of the acting area to the performer's right—the audiences' left.

Stooge seats   Seats normally reserved for members of the cast to use in pretending to be a part of the audience.

Strike   Backstage terminology meaning to remove a unit from the stage.

Teaser   A horizontal masking frame or drapery place upstage of the act curtain to trim the top of the setting.

Twofer   A promotional effort by which two tickets are offered for the price of one.

Traps   Removable sections of the stage floor.

Thrust stage   A stage with seating on three sides.

Velour   A fabric term applying to any material with pile similar to that of velvet.

Wagon   A scene-shifting device consisting of a low platform equipped with casters.

Wing   A hinged unit of scenery placed at the side of the acting area for masking and decorative purposes and painted to represent walls or trees. The offstage side areas are also called the wings.

3. Construction Financing

Because most public assembly facilities are government owned, few have been constructed without the issuance of some type of bond. Although most have been funded by general obligation or revenue bonds, a wide range of financing alternatives can be considered.

Some facilities have been paid for totally or in part by gifts, private investment, or public subscriptions. Other methods of financing include general tax funds, student fees, insurance and bank loans, room taxes, tidelands oil revenue, utility tax, urban renewal, tax increment, and state fair funds. In fact, the methodology may, to some extent, depend on the ingenuity of those responsible for devising the financing scheme.

Such systems, it must be pointed out, present a general picture of possibilities subject to myriad complexities and restrictions created by the variety of governmental jurisdictions, geographic location, and so on.

16

Currently, it appears that funding techniques are divided into three major categories: local mechanisms, state resources, and private investment or public subscription. From time to time federal government programs have been used to underwrite facilities, whole or in part, but the availability of funds is difficult to predict.

GENERAL OBLIGATION BONDS

General obligation bonds are by far the most common method of financing. As implied by their title, general obligation bonds mean just that. Repayment is the responsibility of the entire community and generally means levying a property tax increase. To this is added the problem of obtaining voter approval of the bond issue and the hurdle of selling the public on the idea. In many localities two-thirds of the electorate must approve a general obligation bond issue. In other areas a simple majority will permit its issuance.

As a consequence, general obligation bonds may require a somewhat different type of feasibility study, one that goes beyond a basic analysis of the facility's direct construction costs and operating and maintenance expenses. In effect, one that defines the economic benefits to the governmental jurisdiction from the proposed facility. Some of these benefits include the number of jobs to be created not only by construction but permanently as well, outside revenues to be attracted by the facility, increases in retail sales, benefits to the local economy, and increases in tax revenues.

REVENUE BONDS

The revenue bond for financing enjoys understandingly greater popularity with the taxpayer. In Lennox Moak's, *Administration of Local Government Debt,* the following reasons are listed:

1. It allocates costs to the users ordinarily in relation to the amount of service used. Therefore the taxpayer has relatively little concern with the revenue bond as a taxpayer.
2. There are few, if any, statutory limitations concerning the number of revenue bonds that may be issued.
3. In many government jurisdictions revenue bonds do not require approval of the electorate.
4. There is greater flexibility in arranging the details of the revenue bond issue.

5. When issued without a supplemental general obligation guarantee, the revenue bonds provide a means of financing projects without the downgrading of the full-faith-and-credit pledge.
6. From the standpoint of the investor the revenue bond indenture attempts to provide him with a full measure of protection against adverse management of the revenue-producing facilities.
7. In those states which permit the sale of revenue bonds at non-public sale, some investment bankers and some public officials prefer this route."

The basic function of the revenue bond is to permit the bonding of one or more revenue sources that are not so broad as the credit being pledged under general obligation bonding. It is a more definitive and more restrictive pledge. The municipal bond market operates on the proposition that the holder of a revenue bond has a legal right to look only to the revenues explicitly pledged in support of his bond.

Which revenues can and will be pledged in support of a revenue bond issue is a decision that helps to determine the degree of acceptability of that proposed bond issue in the market, the level of interest rate at which the loan may be secured, and the extent to which excess revenue generated by the undertaking will be available for financing other activities.

In the planning of a revenue bonds issue, it is first necessary to determine the amount of money needed to build a facility. Because revenue projects usually have operating and maintenance expenses associated with them, these requirements must be estimated, and because most revenue projects are essentially government-operated businesses provision must be made for contingencies to meet unexpected expense or losses in revenue.

What are sometimes called "straight" revenue bonds are presumably supported by net revenues derived from facility operations. In other words, a facility funded by revenue bonds should be able to operate in the black or at a profit as it would be described in the private sector.

Revenues from the facility itself, however, are more generally supplemented by those derived from other sources—usually some sort of a tax on lodging, restaurants, admissions, general sales, business and occupational, or liquor.

Whatever the system, competent engineering, management, and financial consultants must be employed and a formal opinion prepared regarding the probable net revenue production of the undertaking.

It is largely on the opinion of these consultants that underwriters and investors decide whether their interest in the bonds being offered is sufficient to warrant purchase. Although some large institutional investors make independent inquiries, many depend on the results of feasibility studies to estimate the net revenues of the facilities being acquired with the proceeds of the bonds.

A review of operating and maintenance costs must involve injection of successive annual increases for inflation and must show a relation to ascending or descending revenue. In the final analysis investors in revenue bonds are looking at coverage—the ratio of net revenue to annual debt service. A minimum coverage of at least 1.5 is almost mandatory for a successful revenue bond issue for a facility of this kind.

If the coverage is below the ratio to attract investors, it may be found necessary to restudy the proposed 20-year maturity with a view to a 30-year maturity schedule. In so doing the average coverage will increase.

Another technique based on revenue bonds has the structure developed and operated by an authority or nonprofit corporation authorized by state-enabling statutes and encompassing certain powers possessed by the jurisdictions that created it.

In such cases the legal right of the government jurisdiction or jurisdictions to enter into a lease agreement would have to be established. In effect, the revenues would be pledged for a long term. If pledges of revenue were based on the general annual revenues of the jurisdiction, there would no doubt be restrictions to prohibit one legislative body from binding future bodies to such long-term commitments.

An example of a lease-purchase plan is the Oakland-Alameda County Coliseum Complex in California. This facility came about in a rather complicated series of legal agreements between the City of Oakland, Alameda County, and a nonprofit corporation.

The corporation, formed to help the city and county to build and operate the facility, sold $25.5 million in bonds to finance construction. The bonds were guaranteed by a long-term operating agreement among the three participants.

Under terms of the operating agreement both the city and county pay $750,000 annually as "rent." The major portion of the $1.5 million thus received is used to retire the debt. The balance and all revenue from the complex are then used to operate the facility. Any funds remaining above these costs revert to the city and county on an annual basis.

At the end of the long-term operating agreement the city and county, which actually own the complex, may choose to extend the contract with the corporation, enter into an agreement with a new corporation, or decide to operate the facility themselves.

On the other hand, at least one state supreme court (Michigan) has ruled that the leases or guarantees provided by the jurisdictions constitute a community's general obligations and must be submitted to the voters for approval.

SPECIAL TAX DISTRICT BONDS

Special tax district bonds, another funding system, assumes that the proposed facility will be in or adjacent to the central business district and will therefore provide special benefits not only to existing businesses but to landowners, where values would be appreciated by the activities of the buildings.

Special districts are generally defined under state laws and any constraints or restrictions must be carefully researched.

TAX INCREMENT BONDS

Another form of revenue bond currently in use is the "tax increment" bond which has commonly been employed to underwrite urban renewal programs. To amortize the bonds the community is permitted to use the difference between the higher tax revenues obtained from the development area after the project has been completed and the lower tax revenues before it was built.

However, in order to employ this process of using the difference between old and new taxes to finance the project, a facility would necessarily have to be built in a "development district" and at the same time additional private taxable investments would have to be made in that district.

STATE OR PROVINCIAL FUNDING RESOURCES

Many state and provincial governments in the United States and Canada have assisted in financing facilities in their metropolitan cities. Political justification has varied, but regardless of the rationale the buildings have been funded and built.

Funding in some cases may not have been total. Some have required matching or at least token participation by the recipient city.

OTHER METHODS

Public assembly facilities have also been linked with other major public improvements in a joint-facility, general obligation bond issue and in numerous cases public assembly facilities have been financed jointly by adjacent or overlapping governmental jurisdictions.

It is not uncommon for projects to be funded by pledges of student activity fees. Obviously such financing plans would be limited to facilities on campus and to fairly large educational institutions.

PUBLIC SUBSCRIPTIONS

The public subscription method of funding is perhaps limited to contributions of all or a major portion of the total capital cost of a facility by a foundation or individual benefactor. Often the building will carry the name of the donor or his organization.

Another form of "public" subscription could, of course, be those facilities that are constructed by private organizations like the Shriners, Knights of Columbus, and American Legion.

PRIVATE INVESTMENT

A number of professional basketball and hockey teams are housed in facilities constructed with private capital, many of which were built by the owners of the sports franchises as a home base for their teams.

By private ownership management is permitted to promote its own shows and control concessions and possibly parking accommodations. The total operation thus greatly increases the prospects for profitability.

Despite their private orientation, some of these buildings owe their existence to an arrangement with the community at large in which land is leased from a park district or other body. In some cases private corporations lease the buildings from their public developers. Although such leases usually cover the public's costs, they can sometimes be set extremely low and thus constitute a form of subsidization.

4. Selecting the Architect

One of the most important decisions the governing body of a public assembly facility must make is the selection of an architect. Some may argue that site selection is more critical, but even in the best of locations poor design can prove to be a continuing embarrassment.

There are several processes by which governmental or private owners can select and retain professional services with respect to the design of a proposed facility. Most are contained in recommendations provided by the American Institute of Architects (AIA) and the American Institute of Planners (AIP).

Elected or appointed officials charged with the selection of an architectural firm should be aware of the implications of such an undertaking. It becomes their responsibility to select professionals who by experience, excellence of design, and dedication will produce a building of the highest quality but still remain within the time and budget constraints imposed by the client.

As a prominent architect and urban planner, points out:

Excellence in building is the by-product of a well-trained architect working for a knowledgeable client who is well informed. This is to say that both parties share in the responsibility, and that a successful project is the result of a successful collaboration between various professional groups and between those groups and the client.

Various methods of selecting an architect are discussed in *The Architect and the Client*, a publication of the American Institute of Architects. Basically three selection methods are open to the client.

Direct selection   The client selects the architect of his choice without comparing him with other architects or other design possibilities.

Comparative selection   The client evaluates the credentials of several architects who he believes may be suited to the project, interviews those in whom he has the most interest, and then selects the one he judges to be the best.

Design competition   The client invites a number of architects to compete equally for the assignment by instituting a competition in which each submits a solution to the building problem. These solutions are judged by a jury of experts which then makes its recommendations to the client. The client then engages the winning architect.

DIRECT SELECTION METHOD

The direct selection method of acquiring an architect is most often used by an individual undertaking a relatively small project. In this method the client selects an architect on the following basis:

1. Reputation
2. Personal acquaintance or recommendation of a friend
3. Recommendation of a former client
4. Recommendation of another architect

The selection is made after informal interviews and is based on his personal desires and overall evaluation of the architect's work and reputation.

The direct selection process has the advantage that it is the least time consuming and least expensive; for small-scale projects the client may feel more comfortable selecting a friend.

There are, however, strong disadvantages in the direct selection process:

- There is no opportunity to investigate alternative design philosophies.
- There is no opportunity to compare excellence of design concept or expertise in a given building type.
- There is no opportunity to negotiate alternative financial arrangements.
- Most important, insofar as public authorities and commissions are concerned, the direct selection process leaves officials open to criticism, accusations of favoritism, or even greater charges.

The size of most public assembly facility projects and their public nature would strongly indicate avoiding the use of the direct selection process.

THE COMPARATIVE SELECTION PROCESS

The comparative selection process is perhaps the most common method of choosing an architect. In essence, one architect is compared with others and the client selects the firm that, in his judgement, is the most qualified.

Usually a system is established under which architectural firms must first qualify for an interview by submitting a description of their capabilities and experiences. The client reviews these submissions and selects those firms that might suit his needs. Representatives of these firms, sometimes referred to as the "short list," are then invited to present the qualifications of their firms at personal interviews.

Among items of information normally solicited from the architect are the following:

1. References from former clients.
2. Size and composition of his office.
3. Ability to devote sufficient time to the project in view of other commitments.
4. A list of similar projects in recent years.

After the committee has interviewed each of the applicants and preferably visited actual buildings built by them it selects the firm that in its opinion is the most capable; it then negotiates the owner-architect agreement and compensation to be paid for architectural services.

If negotiations are successful, the client and architect enter into a legal agreement for professional services. If they fail, the client proceeds to his second choice and attempts to negotiate a contract.

The advantages of selecting an architect by the comparative method are many:

1. The client may compare the levels of expertise offered by the various architects.
2. The client may evaluate more than one architect's approach to the solution of his building program.
3. The client may visit finished buildings of each of the architects and evaluate for himself the architect's abilities.
4. The client has the opportunity to select a single architect from among many.

Naturally there are certain disadvantages as well to the comparative selection method; the process requires more time and the expense is greater.

In many communities, particularly the smaller ones, practical and often political pressures favor the use of locally based architectural firms. This can be implemented in at least two ways under the comparative selection process.

1. Locally based firms can be invited to associate with architects of national or international reputation who have established expertise in projects of similar type or scale and be asked to submit joint qualifications.
2. Locally based firms and national architects can be invited to submit their qualifications individually. One local and one national firm can be chosen by the selection committee and asked to collaborate. If the two firms fail to reach an agreement, the committee can retain the right to drop one or both and bring forward in the order of rank the next firm or firms for similar negotiations.

DESIGN COMPETITION

Design competitions are based on the process by which architectural firms submit solutions to a particular problem and are judged on their comparative excellence. The successful architect is awarded the design of the project. Rules for design competitions were written by the American Institute of Architects.

A client interested in design competition should seek guidance at a local chapter of the AIA. An initial step is the selection of a registered architect to serve as professional adviser. He assists the client, writes the program, advises on the choice of competitors and jury, answers questions, and gives all competitors equal treatment. Strict anonymity is observed to the end that no one is aware of the identity of the creator of any design until the jury makes its final report.

Normally, the program must include a guaranteed contract on acceptable terms to ensure that the winner of the competition will be offered the assignment as architect. Specific provisions to substitute for this requirement are made for public owners. Adequate cash prizes to compensate for the costs of submitting drawings must be awarded to a reasonable number of competitors. In addition to the prizes, fees and expenses should be paid to the professional adviser and members of the jury, the majority of whom would be practicing architects.

A client may wish to combine methods of selection by using, for example, a limited competition held for several equally qualified firms chosen by the comparative selection process.

Advantages of the competition process are as follows:

- For large scale public works the process denotes an element of fairness and openess in which the client makes it known that he is willing to select an architect solely on the basis of excellence in design.
- Design competitions allow firms that might not otherwise be considered to have the opportunity to compete.
- Design competitions allow clients to inspect developed drawings that show many solutions to their building problems before having to commit themselves to a single solution.

There are also disadvantages:

- Well-qualified, established firms may choose not to compete because of the time-consuming requirements.
- Established firms currently engaged in on-going projects may not wish to expend funds speculating on additional commissions through the competition process.
- The competition process is most time consuming for the client. Preparations can take several months, the actual competition period can range from nine months to a year, and time is still required to judge submissions. It is always the possible, also, that it may prove impossible to negotiate a contract with the winner.
- The competition process is costly to both client and competitor.

5. Site Selection

Selection of the site for a public assembly facility, a highly controversial issue in many communities, may prove to be one of the most important decisions of the entire project.

Location studies are often reduced to the comparison of a downtown site with one in a suburban area. Business interests or political pressures are also common factors in most evaluations.

A number of criteria, however, have been developed over the years to assist those who wish to make unbiased appraisals of available sites. Even so, these guidelines become applicable and can be followed only if a clear understanding has been reached regarding the type of facility to be built, its function, and possibly its hoped-for impact on the community.

If a civic center is intended as an "anchor" or catalyst for the redevelopment or rejuvenation of a downtown core area, discussion of any other site becomes completely pointless. If a facility is planned as a community re-source, it serves little purpose to locate the building on a site not readily accessible to the residents of that city or county.

Of note—and perhaps concern—is a 1966 International Association of Auditorium Managers survey in which only 54% of the managers respond-ing rated the location of their facilities as "excellent." Some 38%, however, said their location was "good." Failure to recognize the specific require-ments of the facility and its purpose could be a part of the problem.

Generally speaking, civic centers by their very definition should be as close to the center of a city as possible. The Greeks, it is said, began their cities by first building their theaters and then surrounding them with streets and business premises. This plan anchored the hearts of ancient cities and business activity flowed around these focal points.

Convention centers and exposition halls catering to trade shows display a need for proximity to the bedrooms and dining rooms of hotels and motels. They also require ready access to streets and highways.

Arenas and stadiums must have vast quantities of land not only for the facility and its support activities but also for parking, transit access, and other purposes.

Again speaking on a rather broad basis, a central location for audience support facilities is generally chosen because of its universal accessibility, the greater economic impact that such facilities can have in a downtown location and their significant symbolic relation to the metropolitan area. The suburban location, on the other hand, is favored because parking can be provided at low cost and because land for such sites is usually priced lower.

Extrapolations from an IAAM 1974 survey indicate that the great majority of all public assembly facilities constructed during the last decade—with the obvious exception of stadiums—have been located in what may be termed "downtown" areas.

Five major criteria should be considered in most site location studies.

ACCESSIBILITY

Accessibility may not be *the* most important consideration in the selection of a site but it must be rated *among* the most important factors. An audience support facility should be situated to optimize access from all parts of its service area. Accessibility by automobile, mass transit, and on foot must be analyzed.

Under ideal situations the building or complex should be served by free-ways to carry metropolitan traffic into the vicinity and by a properly integ-rated system of streets to service local traffic. Often overlooked is the fact that arterials linking public assembly facilities must be capable of absorbing "impact" egress traffic loads. Audiences may gather slowly, perhaps over a period of an hour or more, but the entire number usually want to leave simultaneously when the game, entertainment, or meeting has ended.

For convention-oriented facilities pedestrian access is most desirable. Many convention delegates—some for exercise, some for economy—prefer to walk to the conference center rather than use a car or public transportation.

Energy shortages and rising gasoline prices have yet to make their full impact on the transportation habits of millions of North Americans. Gradual shifting to greater use of mass transit is predicted in every quarter, making it mandatory that any successful facility site provide the best possible access and dispersal potentials.

When facilities are designed to meet the specific needs of a community for recreational, educational, artistic, or cultural activities, reasonably heavy traffic from personal transportation can be expected, perhaps creating further consideration in the selection of a site.

PARKING

Although public transportation can be expected to gain in popularity, there can be little question that much of the success or failure of a mass audience facility may depend on the availability of parking space. For many patrons the private automobile is the only means of transportation.

The provision of on-site parking at optimum ratios is, of course, the most desirable, but this ideal situation is, as a rule, reached only in suburban areas. It may become necessary, then, to determine how much off-site parking is available within a short walk (four to five minutes) of the building. The geographic location of the city and its normal weather patterns can also have a strong influence on the distance patrons can be expected to walk from on-street or parking-garage locations.

Parking authorities vary in their estimates, which range from one parking space for each 10 seats or one space for each 100 square feet of exhibit space to as high as one space for each 2.5 seats at a theatrical attraction.

Most active parking-lot operators consider a ratio of one parking space for every three patrons to be a general "rule of thumb." For conventions consumer shows, and similar activities, the ratio may rise to one to five.

The availability of mass transportation can have strong effect on the need for parking space. The size of the city and the driving habits of its citizens must also be taken into consideration.

SUPPORT SERVICES

Support services such as hotels, motels, restaurants, lounges, service stations, and possibly places of entertainment are necessary adjuncts to the successful public assembly facility.

Obviously out-of-town convention delegates will require overnight accommodations—the nearer the better. Even if the facility provides food and beverage service, seldom will it be capable of meeting the total requirements, especially when sports or large-audience events are scheduled.

Because these services can be expected to receive the initial or direct benefit of spending by those using the facility, the relation of site to them can have great affect on the economy of the community; for example, a person may decide to have dinner at a nearby restaurant if he can later walk to the theater; a convention delegate traveling by car may have it serviced at a local station before leaving the community.

ECONOMIC AND ESTHETIC IMPACT

Public assembly facilities can be expected to generate several types of economic activity. Perhaps the most clearly identifiable example is money spent by convention delegates. Their spending patterns have been the subject of intensive study by the International Association of Convention and Visitors Bureaus.

This survey is updated periodically, and although dollar amounts continue to reflect inflationary trends the distribution shows little variation. A typical spread of the "convention dollar" (based on 804 conventions in 54 cities) indicates that the average delegate spends $100 on the following items:

Hotel rooms and incidentals	$37.66
Hotel restaurants	15.99
Other restaurants	16.18
Beverages	6.01
Retail stores (not food)	10.28
Local transportation, sight-seeing, theaters	3.82
Night clubs, sports events	3.51
Automobile service	1.75
All other items	4.80
	$100.00

Source: International Association of Convention and Visitors Bureaus, 1973

Economically, this impact on the community becomes even more impressive when the "multiplier" effect of these new dollars is considered. Some individuals, discussing the "multiplier," like to assign figures ranging from 3 to 7 and some go even higher with little evidence to substantiate their claims. Perhaps the most generally accepted and supportable multiplier figure is 3; thus $20 million in first-round spending can be reasonably expected to increase to $60 million in any particular city, state, or area.

Generally speaking, the multiplier is said to be the estimated number of times a given dollar will "turn over" before eventually leaving the area in which it was first spent.

Although the convention dollar is the most evident and traceable, there can be little doubt that a busy mass audience facility offering a steady schedule of attractions will also generate additional spending among local and area residents, thus contributing to the general economy.

Finally, there is the money spent by performers, athletes, and exhibitors at the events in which they are involved. Needless to say, the economic benefits derived from the latter sources are often far greater when the facility is centrally located—this because of its proximity to establishments that offer goods and services.

Whether the term "esthetic impact" is proper or whether it should be "community pride" or "symbolism" may depend on the situation. The effect is an intangible but highly important element in determining the location for a public assembly facility.

Publicly or privately financed, these buildings represent a substantial investment. As centers of civic interest and symbolic of community achievement and progress they may perhaps be the most active of any public "utility." Citizens in general develop great pride in "their" auditorium, music hall, or stadium and show great satisfaction in its becoming a must-see attraction on all city tours. As a focal point of the community the total development of its site and neighboring environment are of virtually equal importance. It follows therefore that any area chosen should be capable of such development.

SITE ADAPTABILITY, AVAILABILITY, AND COST

A serious problem in the selection of the proper location for a public assembly facility is the availability (at a reasonable cost) of sufficient land for the building or complex and on-site parking. The only adequate land area may reveal unfavorable soil conditions for normal construction.

Although suburban sites may be easier to locate and more readily obtainable, urban renewal and other publicly assisted land clearance techniques have often been employed to provide sufficient space in downtown locations.

Land costs are another consideration. Construction in suburban locations normally calls for sufficient parking for all possible events, thus increasing the total volume of land required. This parking space is normally used only by the occupants of the facility.

Conversely, construction in a downtown location can mean that the facility can utilize both on-street and existing parking accommodations. This could, of course, substantially reduce the amount of land required.

The following is a summary of criteria recommended by the International Association of Auditorium Managers and several nationally recognized management and economic consultants:

Accessibility

- Streets and highways—ingress and egress
- Transit access
- Pedestrian access

Parking

- On-site parking capabilities
- Off-site parking capabilities

Support Services

- Proximity to hotels, motels, restaurants
- Proximity to retail stores
- Proximity to entertainment/recreational attractions

Economic Impact

- Potential for attracting "outside" dollars
- Potential for generation of local spending
- Attraction for additional public and private investment.
- Community "image" or pride

Site Adaptability, Availability, and Cost

- Site size
- Possibility of acquisition of land
- Site preparation
- Utilities
- Site cost
- Possibility of future expansion

6. Arenas and Coliseums

According to some dictionaries, an arena is "the central space for contestants," a coliseum is "a large building or stadium for sports events, shows, and exhibitions."

In some American cities the roofed buildings in which spectators witness athletic contests and mass entertainments are called gardens, auditoriums, fieldhouses, assembly halls, pavilions, and even civic centers.

For purposes of this chapter, then, an arena or coliseum is a totally enclosed structure housing a rectangular playing floor of sufficient dimension to accommodate basketball or hockey and surrounded on two or more sides by elevated seating for spectators.

More than 200 public assembly facilities of this type exist in the United States and Canada today and have become an integral part of daily life in most cities of any substantial size. Others are located in major population centers throughout the world and many more are under construction or on the drawing boards.

Among the sports events that dominate the schedules in most arenas and coliseums basketball and hockey enjoy the greatest acceptance. Rock concerts are a close second and the leader in some cities. Ice shows, circuses, rodeos, contemporary music, tennis, indoor track, and a score of other activities all vie for their share of the public's time and ticket dollars.

Basic in the design and function of the arena is a central floor space with virtually unlimited load capacity. Size is normally dictated by primary function, but inclusion of an ice sheet 85 feet wide by 200 feet long for hockey suggests a more or less standard floor size. Surrounding the ice surface may be sufficient floor space for a portable track. The establishment of these parameters usually results in a facility capable of handling most currently common activities.

Perhaps the singular difference between European and North American arenas has been the installation of permanent bicycle tracks in the European facilities. In general, these tracks limit seating capacity and hamper use of the buildings for many other events. Some observers predict that the gradual decline in the popularity of bicycle racing will eliminate permanent tracks in future multipurpose buildings on the Continent.

Spectator seating capacities range from a few thousand to about 20,000 at some of the newer facilities in major population centers. Virtually all arenas offer individual seating, as opposed to bleacher seating, and, except in Europe, a majority now provide chairs with padded seats and backs. Most seats are permanently mounted to concrete risers.

Design of the seat form normally requires a concrete wall or bulkhead to which the telescoping risers are secured. Chairs are usually either folding and movable or permanently-affixed folddown seats. Few of these risers or tribunes, as they are called in Europe, are seen there.

Basketball and hockey have already been mentioned and it is probably for these two sports that most of the arenas in the United States and Canada have been built. The two activities, however, actually represent only a small part of the program of the average building. It is this alternative use factor, studies have shown, that make arena balance sheets more favorable than those of many stadiums.

Other sports activities common to or possible in arenas:

- Indoor track
- Box lacrosse
- Indoor soccer
- Boxing
- Wrestling

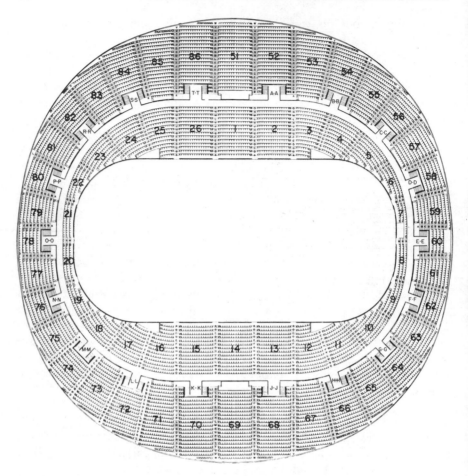

Four basic seating configurations are common in the operational patterns of most multi-purpose arenas.

Figure 1   shows the permanent seating with telescoping risers, either stacked or removed. This setup is used for exhibits, dances, or any activity that requires maximum floor space. An ice hockey setup would be similar with perhaps portable seating added around the rink.

- Rodeo
- Horse shows
- Motorcycle racing
- Bicycle racing
- Handball
- Volleyball
- Gymnastics
- Closed-circuit telecasts

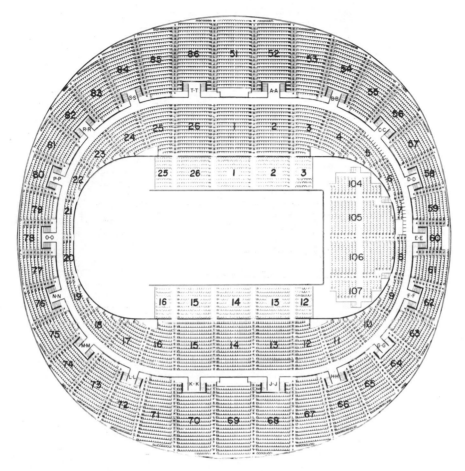

Figure 2   shows portable seating on the sides and one end but with space left open for the curtains and scenery of an ice show.

Demanding substantial time frames in most arenas is a wide variety of "family shows" and concerts of contemporary music:

• Ice shows
• Circuses
• Local pageants or spectaculars
• Rock music concerts
• Country/western concerts
• Gospel sings
• Popular music concerts
• Square dances

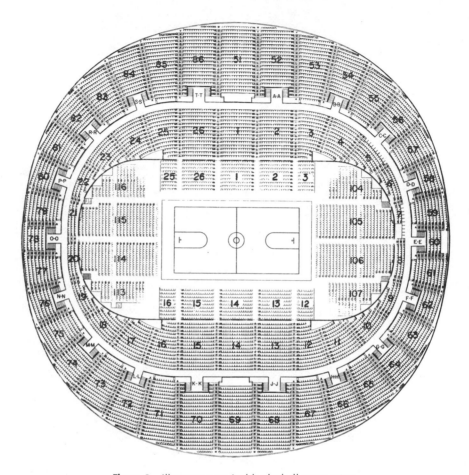

Figure 3   illustrates a typical basketball game setup.

Depending on adjacent facilities and other conditions, the arena floor may also be the site of a number of exhibits and trade shows:

- Home shows
- Automobile shows
- Dog shows
- Boat shows
- Sport shows
- Roadster shows
- Motorcycle shows
- Flower and garden shows

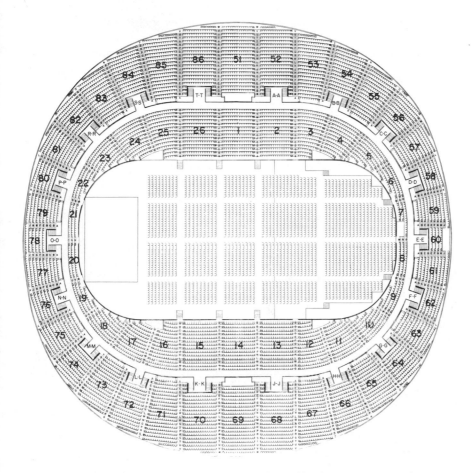

Figure 4 shows the arena floor with one of several possible chair arrangements for a convention or concert.

- Recreational vehicle shows
- Home furnishing shows
- Antique shows

Conventions, high school and university activities, and religious gatherings are other potential candidates for the use of arenas and their large seating capacities.

Flexibility therefore must be the keynote in all planning of this nature. The needs of athletes and entertainers—as well as audiences—must be considered. The ability of management to change the setup rapidly from the accommodation of one purpose to that of another yields a truly functional building.

If an ice rink is an integral feature of the arena, a concrete floor is dictated. Concrete is also the most versatile for multipurpose facilities. In buildings intended for more specific purposes, such as basketball or tennis, hardwood or possibly "Tartan"-like materials may be an alternate choice.

Space for an ice melting pit is of great importance for lowering an arena's cost of operation and for increasing scheduling capabilities. Its location should, of course, be on the immediate perimeter of the ice rink, where its cover will not interfere with other building functions.

Other provisions in the floor design must be made for hockey dasher anchors, circus and other show tie-offs, conduits for scoreboard cables, and other timing devices. Large access doors into the arena are vital for truck deliveries.

At one end of the arena, normally referred to as "backstage," space must be reserved for power sources and other utilities. Substantial area is needed to accommodate temporary ice shows, circuses, and other events. It is also in this backstage area that offices, dressing rooms, and showers are located. A detailed discussion of dressing rooms is included in a later chapter.

Storage requirements for arena-oriented equipment are substantial. As an example, space may be needed to accommodate a portable basketball court, an ice floor cover, running track, folding chairs, basketball backstops, hockey dashers and glass screens, hockey goals, ice resurfacing machines, ice removal equipment, forklift trucks, material-handling equipment, portable staging, portable risers, steps, floor scrubbers, and vacuum cleaners. Quantification of storage space should be carefully researched; it may, however, depend to some degree on accessibility, for all storage should be located with strong reference to the arena floor in the interest of rapid shifting of equipment.

Ceiling heights are normally 50 feet or more; many exceed 65 feet. Needless to say, virtually all arenas today have clear span design to avoid obstruction of vision from any seat in the house.

The arena ceiling must be designed to support the extremely heavy weight of a scoreboard and possibly a message center. In addition, many speaker clusters are located above center floor in conjunction with the scoreboards.

Provision must also be made for tie-offs in the ceiling structure to accommodate rigging as well as lighting equipment. Other necessities include spotlight balconies, sound and light consoles, and press boxes.

Of special interest to arena operations is easy and safe access to all portions of the roof or ceiling area. Often, during a show, there may be as many workers overhead as on the floor. Catwalks should be accessible and free from restrictive ducts or other incumbrances. In most modern arenas all lighting fixtures can be easily reached from the catwalks for adjustment, maintenance, or replacement. Although sports activities normally call for broad or general lighting, many entertainment events find an ever-increasing need for controlled lighting to create special effects or to focus audience attention.

On the subject of lighting, any arena in which the presentation of shows is contemplated will require black-out or at least darkening capabilities. The daytime or matinee performances of many events would be virtually impossible, or at least highly undesirable, unless the house could be darkened for scenery changes and cast placement. This condition brings with it the need for consideration of aisle safety lights in those communities in which fire and/or safety codes require them.

Admission control and security are extremely important to successful arena operation. This subject is somewhat complex and is discussed in detail in Chapter 12. The same comment applies to first aid rooms, concessions, and public skating.

Last, it should be stressed that the inter relation of assigned spaces within the arena is of vital importance and cannot be overlooked if the building is to function properly.

Figures 5 to 14 show examples of arenas located throughout the United States.

Figure 5. Full-size aircraft complete with other decorations for attention in a typical sports show setup on an arena floor. In many communities the arena floor must serve for exhibitions as well as sports and entertainment.

Figure 6. Perhaps the best known arena in the world is Madison Square Garden in the heart of New York. Home of the New York Knicks (National Basketball Association) and the New York Rangers (National Hockey League), the Garden provides 17,218 permanent and 2,420 portable seats.

Figure 7. The use of telescoping risers and folding chairs boosts the seating capacity of Madison Square Garden to more than 19,000 for basketball. In addition to the basketball setup, this photograph also gives an excellent view of the unique ceiling structure.

Figure 8. Designed for conventions, entertainment, and boxing more than basketball and hockey, the Las Vegas Convention Center is an interesting example of a round arena. The building contains 4392 permanent seats and can accommodate approximately 3000 portable chairs. (Las Vegas News Bureau.)

Figure 9. Of great importance to most arenas are the rent and other revenues from rock music concerts. This photograph shows the Forum in Inglewood, California, set up for a Cat Stevens concert. Note the additional speakers on stage, at both sides, and at the rear of the hall.

Figure 10. Unique in many respects is the Assembly Hall at the University of Illinois in Champaign. Designed to serve both sports and entertainment, the building consists of two concrete bowls placed face to face. One is the seat bowl, the other the roof bowl or dome. They measure 400 feet across, thus making the dome one of the largest in the world.

Figure 11. The University of Illinois Assembly Hall provides 16,000 permanent seats for basketball and other sports events. Here the floor of the huge arena is shown with a portable rink prepared for a professional ice show. The structure suspended from the ceiling accommodates special lighting, public address speakers, and rigging for curtains.

Figure 12.   Here the University of Illinois Assembly Hall presents a more dignified theatrical appearance. A thrust stage and curtains are in place. Concerts, musicals, operas, and ballets are presented in the theater quadrant of the hall which seats 4200 persons. The overhead grid supports 32 electronically operated battens for handling scenery and curtains.

Figure 13. Called "The Coliseum," this arena was opened in the mid-1970s in Richfield Township, near Cleveland, Ohio. The photograph illustrates a facility with hockey dashers and glass screens in place but with the floor covered and a basketball court in place. Most arenas find it advantageous to leave the ice sheet undisturbed as much as possible, covering the ice for basketball and other events during the hockey season.

Figure 14. Perhaps better known as a convention center than a sports facility is Cobo Hall, located in downtown Detroit. The arena is unique in the high degree of design and finish accorded one end of the building. The same comment applies to the ceiling. Cobo Hall has 9561 permanent seats and can accommodate 2396 portable chairs. (City of Detroit photo.)

7. Theaters, Auditoriums, and Concert Halls

A theater has been described as "a building especially adapted to dramatic, operatic or spectacular representations . . . a playhouse." The form, shape, size and seating capacities of such structures may well be as varied as their uses. Figures 15 to 19 show five possible theatrical arrangements.

It is generally agreed that no single size of theater will fit the needs of all performances. As a result, construction in recent years has given us complexes like Lincoln Center for the Performing Arts in New York, John F. Kennedy Center in Washington, and the Music Center of the County of Los Angeles in which separate but adjacent facilities of varying seating capacities have been provided to accommodate the different requirements.

Certain basic types and sizes of theater, however, appear to have evolved over the years.

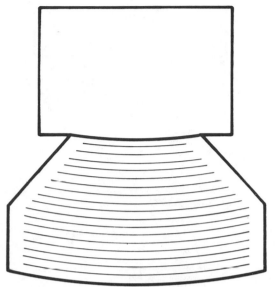

Figure 15.   Proscenium Theater. Perhaps the most familiar form is the proscenium theater, a facility adaptable to traditional types of drama and audiovisual presentations. It is less acceptable for concert presentations because of the stagehouse. This particular sketch illustrates the seating in continental form. The use of more conventional aisles, however, would not basically affect the overall shape of the theater.

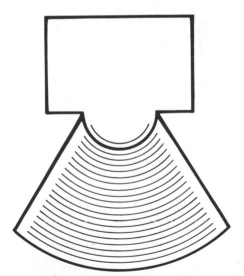

Figure 16.   Thrust Proscenium Theater. This form has a stagehouse and acting area of nominal size. In addition, it has a thrust stage in front of the proscenium which projects into the audience at a wide fan angle of approximately 90 degrees. This projection realizes full use of the thrust forestage while still providing for stage sets and acting areas within the frame of the proscenium. This type of theater provides an intimate setting with a high degree of flexibility for a wide range of productions.

49

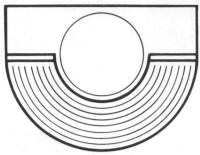

Figure 17. Thrust Stage Theater. In this form the audience encircles the stage at 180 degrees. There may be a proscenium opening with a shallow stage, but because of the wide encirclement by the audience it is effective only to a limited depth. This type of theater is adaptable to contemporary drama forms, single performers, or small casts.

Figure 18. Frameless Proscenium Theater. This theater places the audience and the acting area in the same visual space without apparent separation of the proscenium. It is generally a linear space in which the stage is located at one end and the audience faces it in a narrow fan.

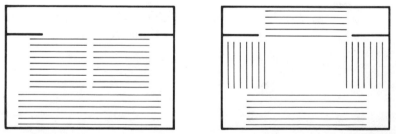

Figure 19. Multiform Experimental Theater. This theater provides the maximum flexibility of seating arrangements, acting area, scenery placement, lighting, and acoustical control. The two sketches show possibilities of change from a proscenium to an arena stage. It offers extreme flexibility to the presentation of large casts before small audiences and is highly desirable as a rehearsal facility which may have multiple uses. This type of theater requires considerable labor in changeover from one form to the other both in setup and striking.

CONCERT HALLS

Perhaps the most popular theater size for the average community is the concert hall or "auditorium." Seating capacities usually fall somewhere between 2500 and 3500. A few examples are substantially higher but apparently are the exception.

At one time most public audience support facilities, whether arenas, theaters, or exhibition halls, were referred to as "auditoriums." For our purposes, however, "auditoriums" are considered to be theater-type structures with fixed seating on a sloping floor facing a permanent, proscenium stage.

Such facilities are primarily oriented toward cultural events, especially music. They appear to suit the needs of grand opera and symphony and touring or "Broadway" musicals. These theaters are highly favored by commercial promoters who point out that when capacities are substantially lower than 3000 seats it becomes unprofitable to present many traveling attractions.

With a larger capacity, however, the distance of a theater's rear seats from the stage or the sight lines of its side seats are inevitably less than ideal. Acoustics for some presentations may be questionable, for amateur and semiprofessional groups would probably lack the projection to fill the hall. The cost of operating the larger theaters is substantially greater and attractions capable of filling such high-capacity facilities are few—particularly in smaller communities.

On the lower side of the scale the 2500-seat houses appear to be more popular. Halls of this size are likely to be more satisfactory acoustically and to fit the needs of modern dance, musical comedy, and ballet. Some theater consultants contend that classical drama can successfully play theaters with 2500 seats, provided that all are within 75 feet of the stage.

The possibility of fully flexible all-purpose theaters has been explored in many communities. Mechanical devices to seal off balconies or otherwise reduce the seating area have made it possible to combine a concert hall and theater. Little compromise has been reached, however, between the different demands of drama and music because acoustical treatment that is good for one may possibly be unsatisfactory for the other.

The situation is well summarized in a report of the Twentieth Century Fund Task Force on Performing Arts Centers, *"Bricks, Mortar and the Performing Arts"*:

Every reduction in seating capacity means, however, a reduction in the income from booking an extremely popular artist or event, and from the subscription series featuring such artists or events. There is, in other words, a trade-off. Smaller theaters are usually less expensive to build and maintain, and will make fewer demands on the artists. They are likely to be used more often, reducing the subsidy required by the theater itself. But the reduced seating capacity means increased subsidy for symphony orchestras and opera or ballet companies which play the house, and may make it impossible to book major touring attractions at all. In planning a smaller theater, sponsoring groups should also plan an annual subsidy to make possible the importation of nationally recognized ensembles and soloists whose appearances stimulate a necessary excitement in the artistic life of a city (Twentieth Century Fund, 1970).

THEATERS AND PLAYHOUSES

Here again, terminologies are cloudy, for many facilities provide seating ranging downward from the 2500-person mark to around 1200.

Some of these halls are architectural showplaces and must be considered ideal for concerts, recitals, and plays often referred to as "legitimate" theater. Most of the Broadway playhouses fall into this smaller category.

One experienced consultant states:

The theater is a specialized auditorium and emphasizes the production of stage shows rather than general utilization for cultural events. Theaters usually have a maximum seating capacity of around 1,200 persons and may seat as few as 200 to 300. The emphasis in a theater is on good production facilities and physical rapport between audience and performer.

Economically, however, theaters in the 1200-seat range are rarely profitable except in large population centers. Substantial local uses for smaller auditoriums and theaters are found in many communities, but the lack of capacity prohibits their use by major touring attractions or highly paid popular artists.

The 1200-seat theater in the average-size community will probably require extensive subsidization. Shows that can be afforded commercially often fail to draw full houses except in the most unusual circumstances. Many experienced facility managers recommend that beyond 800 seats the next operationally sound step for a publicly owned theater is not less than 2400 to 2500 seats.

Little Theaters

Most of the regional repertory theaters operate in houses that seat no more than 800 and some dramatic groups, playing in smaller communities, have been most successful in facilities accommodating as few as 350 to 375 persons.

Smaller theaters have also proved to be popular for a wide variety of activities that includes recitals and certain one-artist shows. It is interesting to note that in most cities the schedules of such facilities are extremely crowded.

Outdoor Theaters

Outdoor facilities may range from the traditional Shakespearean theaters found in several cities throughout the United States and Canada to the spaciousness of such places as Red Rocks Theater in Denver, Forest Park Theater in St. Louis, or the Concord Pavilion in Concord, California.

Experimental Theaters

Sometimes called "black boxes," experimental or multi-form theaters are usually constructed with flat floors to permit arrangement of portable seating and staging in any manner desired. Lighting is also primarily ceiling-hung to provide the greatest possible flexibility.

Theater Design

Professional consultants with expertise in planning, design, and construction are of utmost importance to the successful development of theatrical facilities and should be allowed access to the owner or governmental agency responsible for the project as well as to the architects. Their opinions on questions of use and cost should be overruled only after the most carefully considered discussions.

Management matters, including the potential marketing of the facility plus projected operational costs and administrative plans, must be taken into consideration.

Coupled with the input of the theater consultant is usually the need for the advice and direction of an experienced acoustician to assist the consultant who may not be qualified in this particular field.

Utilization of such expertise in a carefully developed team can do much to ensure the creation of a facility that will more closely meet the purpose for which it was designed.

Figures 20 to 33 show various examples of theaters, auditoriums, and concert halls.

Figure 20. Dorothy Chandler Pavilion is the largest of three theaters in The Music Center of the County of Los Angeles. The Chandler Pavilion seats 3197 and accommodates symphony, grand opera, musical comedy, and ballet. It is 330 feet long, 252 wide, and is surrounded by fluted columns that extend the full height of 92 feet.

Figure 21. In the center of the pool gracing the plaza of The Music Center of the County of Los Angeles is the Jacques Lipchitz masterwork, "Peace on Earth." In the background is the Mark Taper Forum, joined by a colonnade to the Ahmanson Theatre directly behind it. The Forum, the smallest of the three theaters, seats 742 in a semicircular arrangement. It is designed to accomodate intimate drama, recitals, chamber music, lectures, and civic-cultural events.

Figure 22. The Ahmanson Theater is more modern in design than the Dorothy Chandler Pavilion. The Ahmanson Theater, the midsize facility in the theater complex, provides seating for 2071 patrons. The entire front wall is faced with smoky glass reflecting the Pavilion, and the Forum, smallest of the theaters.

Figure 23. Grady Gammage Memorial Auditorium on the campus of Arizona State University in Tempe was the last of Frank Lloyd Wright's major architectural designs. Illuminated foyers, colonnades, and vaulted bridges reflect the soft colors of the Arizona desert. The auditorium stands 80 feet high. (Courtesy of ASU Photo Service.)

Figure 24. Unique in Grady Gammage Memorial Auditorium is the 145-foot-wide grand tier which spans the theater from side to side without touching the rear wall and enhances the facility's acoustical excellence. Total seating capacity is 3019. The grand tier seats 601 patrons and the balcony accommodates 668. The most distant balcony seat is only 115 feet from the forestage. Seating is continental with no radial aisles. (Courtesy of Frank Lloyd Wright Foundation.)

Figure 25. unique and attractive treatment of the stage house is seen in the design of the Spokane Opera House. Seating 2,700 persons, the theater was constructed as a feature of Expo '74. Adjoining the Opera House is the 40,000 square foot Convention Center.

Figure 26. Lincoln Center for the Performing Arts is the most expansive array of facilities in North America and perhaps the entire world. Located on a 14-acre site on Manhattan's upper west side, this complex is comprised of Avery Fisher Hall, the New York State Theater, the Metropolitan Opera House, the Vivian Beaumont and Mitzi E. Newhouse theaters, the Juilliard School, Alice Tully Hall, The New York Public Library at Lincoln Center, the Library & Museum of the Performing Arts, the Guggenheim Bandshell, and Damrosch Park. Here is shown Avery Fisher Hall, which opened in September 1962 and was the first building to be completed at the Center. (Photograph by Ezra Stoller Associates.)

Figure 27. This view of the Metropolitan Opera House, which opened in September 1966, shows the relationship of three of the major theaters at Lincoln Center for the Performing Arts. A part of the New York State Theater can be seen on the left and a portion of Avery Fisher Hall, on the right. (Courtesy of GTE Sylvania Inc. Photograph by Peter Fink.)

Figure 28. After many problems with the acoustical properties of Avery Fisher Hall, the 2742-seat auditorium was reconstructed and reopened in October 1976. The old auditorium was removed back to the inner structure of the walls, ceiling, and floor, and a totally different auditorium was built in the cleared space. This photograph shows the new hall. (Photograph by Sandor Acs.)

Figure 29. The beautiful interior of the New York State Theater is illustrated in this photograph which shows the flowing lines of the five balcony tiers. The theater seats 2729 persons. (Photograph by Ezra Stoller Associates.)

Figure 30. A performer fortunate enough and with sufficient talent would have this view from the stage of the 2800-seat Metropolitan Opera House at Lincoln Center for the Performing Arts. (Lincoln Center for the Performing Arts, Inc. Photograph by Bob Serating.)

Figure 31. The second of the buildings to be completed in Lincoln Center for the Performing Arts was the New York State Theater designed by Philip Johnson. This facility, home of the City Center of Music and Drama's New York City Ballet and New York City Opera companies, open in April 1964. In the foreground is the Lincoln Center Foundation, also designed by Johnson. (Photograph by Ezra Stoller Associates.)

Figure 32. This photo of the 1140-seat auditorium of the Vivian Beaumont Theater at Lincoln Center is an excellent example of the stage in its thrust position. This theater serves as the permanent home of the Repertory Theater of Lincoln Center. It opened in October 1965. (Lincoln Center for the Performing Arts, Inc. Photograph by Ezra Stoller Associates.)

Figure 33. Smallest of the facilities at Lincoln Center Alice Tully Hall has 1096 seats. Looking toward the stage the view is of the auditorium which is located in the Juilliard School building. This intimate hall, with its basswood walls and lively colored seats, was designed specifically for chamber music and recitals. The Chamber Music Society of Lincoln Center is the resident company. (Photo by Ezra Stoller Associates.)

8. Exhibition Halls

Because of its primary function, the architectural program for an exhibition hall ideally demands a boxlike structure of unlimited floor loads, unhampered free space, and a ceiling height of not less than 25 feet.

The size of the proposed display hall will depend on many factors. Some guidelines can, however, be employed to help in this critical decision.

If the primary purpose of the hall is to cater to state and regional conventions, surveys indicate that such groups require an average of 12,500 net square feet. Still further research indicates that nearly 80% of all convention displays currently use fewer than 10,000 net square feet. This leads to the conclusion that a facility of 20,000 to 25,000 gross square feet would be adequate to serve that segment of the market. (Figures are extrapolated from Market Survey Reports of *Association Management* and Market Report Data published by *Meetings & Conventions*.)

General rule-of-thumb formulas for the arrangement of exhibits assume that only 50 to 60% of the gross square footage of a hall can be utilized. The balance must be assigned to aisle space, fire and emergency exits, audience support facilities, and other purposes. It is often necessary also to devote considerable space to registration areas and information desks.

Few consumer shows can operate profitably on fewer than 50,000 gross square feet of exhibit space, and many of the major show management organizations will consider nothing smaller than 100,000 square feet.

Modern exhibition buildings in major convention cities have continued to expand over the years in direct response to specific needs. A number of halls have reached the 300,000 square foot mark and further expansion may be planned.

Halls of rectangular shape are favored for the maximum development of booth layouts. A square hall apparently presents few, if any, problems, but round buildings or those with diagonal corners are considered most difficult for standard arrangements.

The average show will offer its exhibitors booth space 10 feet wide and 8 or 10 feet deep, depending on the total available space and the configurations. Aisles are normally 10 to 12 feet wide. (see Figures 34 and 35).

Exhibit booths are customarily of pipe-and-drape construction, 8 feet high at the rear and with 4-foot railings along each side. Drapes are usually bengaline or some similar hard-finish, low-cost fabric, which ideally should resist creasing or its folds should hang out rapidly (see Figure 36).

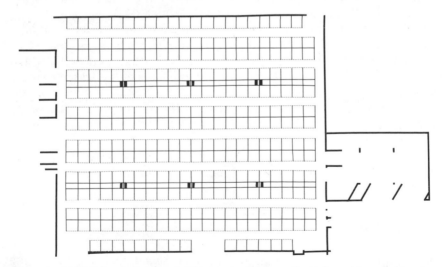

Figure 34. Exhibit Booth Layouts. Exhibit booths are normally 10 feet wide and either 8 or 10 feet deep. Depending on many factors, a show manager may elect to develop his show layout with all major aisles opening to the hall entrance or with aisles leading to the sides of the hall. This setup accommodates 300 standard booths.

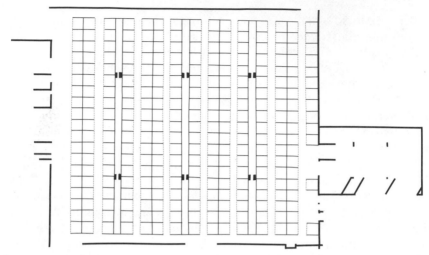

Figure 35.   The layout in Figure 35 provides for 279 booths. A "rule-of-thumb" states that approximately 60% of an exhibition hall's square footage is usable or salable space. The approximate size of the building in Figures 34 and 35 is 50,000 square feet.

In the United States and Canada drape equipment is normally provided by a professional show decorator under a rental agreement with the sponsoring association. In some communities, however, booths are owned by the convention hall management and leased to exhibitors.

Common practice calls for show management to provide each exhibitor with drapes and a duplex 110-volt electrical outlet. He may also be given a standard identification sign. All other items in the booth are either brought to the hall by the exhibitor or rented for the duration of the show from the decorator.

Some trends to free-form exhibit spaces with curvilinear aisles or salon space, for which the exhibitor reserves a block of 500 to 1000 square feet or more, have been noted but are still in the minority.

With reference to supporting posts, none is best—the fewer the better. If posts prove to be necessary, their location on 30-foot modules appear to be most common and acceptable.

DIVIDER WALLS

Movable panel walls permit the reduction or alteration of the size of the exhibition area and serve to increase the flexibility of the facility.

Use of divider walls make it possible to lease space simultaneously for two or more activities; they also create storage areas for crates if all the space is not required for exhibits and make smaller halls possible as needed.

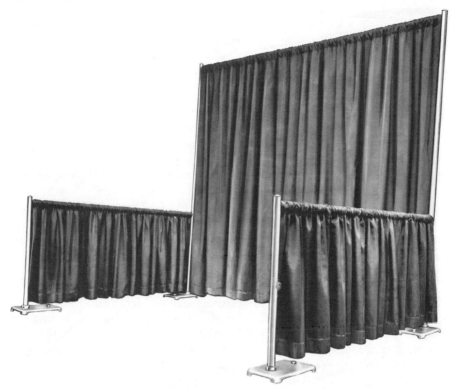

Figure 36. Display booths for exhibitions are normally created by the use of pipe and drape equipment. Booths are most commonly 10 feet wide and 8 or 10 feet deep. Height is normally fixed at 8 feet at the rear and 4 feet on the sides. Aluminum tubing is telescopic for flexibility and storage. (Lawrence Metal Products.)

Plans for the use of movable walls must include the accommodation of entrances and exits which relate to the various configurations that can be created. Systems for the movement of equipment and personnel from one area to another must also be considered. If food and beverage service is contemplated, proper access to and screening from serving areas will be required.

Often additional trackage for the walls by which the hall can be divided into three or four sections, as needed, is planned for two or more locations. Such flexibility can be of great value.

Movable walls must be reasonably soundproof and at the same time provide proper security. The performance of this equipment depends on careful planning by the architect and his mechanical engineers or consultants; close coordination with representatives of the manufacturers of panel walls or similar closures is also required.

Provision must also be made for adequate storage. For some types of movable wall this space often proves to be substantial.

FLOORS, CEILINGS, AND WALLS

The floor of an exhibit hall is subjected to extremely hard use. Motorized vehicles leave rubber marks, packing crates scratch the surface, and exhibitors frequently spill paint and other liquids. The most economical and durable floor is concrete.

Although unlimited floor loads are recommended few producers demand more than 300 to 350 pounds per square foot.

Ceiling heights should ideally be at least 25 feet. This height permits easy access of over-the-road trucks, most heavy commercial or construction equipment, and multilevel booths. Further, when platforms are introduced into the hall, the higher ceiling becomes less restrictive of the types of entertainment or other activity that may be presented.

Ceiling heights much in excess of 25 feet can present handicaps, particularly if utilities are to be provided from overhead. Wall surface materials should be as durable as possible, for all surfaces are subjected to frequent scratching and scraping by vehicles and packing crates. Exhibitors also often use wall surfaces for displaying signs and advertising materials. When possible, a tack strip or eye bolts installed at the ceiling line of all walls reduces wall damage. The tack strip of course, should be replaceable.

When wall corners are exposed to vehicular traffic, such as forklift trucks, electric carts, or scrub machines, it is recommended that steel protectors be provided.

In regard to design and color, wall surfaces should be treated to avoid interference with show themes, color, and lighting. Many show managers and decorators now drape all walls from floor to ceiling to present uniformity in appearance and design.

Constant custodial work is required during exhibit hours. In addition, frequent spillages and other minor problems require immediate attention. With these facts in mind, the location of janitor's closets at convenient points in the exhibition hall is helpful.

LIGHTING

Good lighting is essential to show management and exhibitors alike. Most halls are illuminated with fluorescent, mercury-vapor or similar lights and although dimmers are not necessarily required some method of reducing the light level by switch is needed.

Ground-level windows should be avoided. During ingress and egress of shows and occasionally when empty the appearance of exhibit halls is unsightly and lacking in good housekeeping. Sunlight through windows fades the decorator's equipment, washes out the color and lighting of many exhibits, distracts exhibit viewers, and conveys excessive heat.

Further, display booths are normally arranged with draped backs to the window walls, a practice that creates a less than inviting picture from the outside.

Although specific proof may be lacking, windows may create security problems for show management during off hours.

If windows are deemed mandatory for design or esthetic purposes, adequate blackout shades must be provided.

UTILITIES

In addition to 110- and 220-volt power, exhibitors will require water, gas, compressed air, telephone service, and some floor drains. It is also considered necessary to provide at least a limited capability for exhausting fumes when gasoline engines or other types of odor-producing equipment are demonstrated.

Power for exhibitors has been distributed in a variety of systems, depending on structural handicaps and opportunity. In some facilities energy is delivered by overhead busses, in others through tunnels under the exhibit hall floor, and in still others from sources located in major roof support pillars. When the hall is constructed over a basement or underground garage, excellent distribution systems have been developed with floor accesses.

Normal practice calls for the facility to provide heavy power lines at convenient locations throughout the hall. From these sources either the show or house electrician will connect distribution boxes from which to run the harness that supplies individual booths. Both closed-circuit and broadcast television accommodations are required.

If possible, heating and/or air-conditioning units should be positioned to avoid direct blowing of air on any area in which exhibits may be erected.

Because loading doors remain open during most of the ingress time immediately preceding opening day, heating equipment should provide reasonably quick recovery of temperature for the comfort of exhibitors and visitors. Some form of heat or "air curtain" near the loading doors is recommended.

LOADING FACILITIES

Special attention must be paid to loading and unloading facilities because moving a show in and out rapidly may be a primary factor in the acceptance or rejection of a particular event. Ingress/egress speed is equally important to the financial welfare of show management and drayage contractor.

If at all possible, receiving facilities for the building should be provided in addition to those available for the delivery of exhibit materials.

The desirability of loading and unloading directly on the floor will depend on the size and nature of the exhibit. Large conventions normally see most materials being shipped to a common warehouse and then brought to the exhibition hall in large vans. Regional or locally oriented shows usually attract a number of smaller trucking companies in the area.

Several large doors should provide easy access to the exhibit hall floor. In addition, a loading dock is highly recommended. For agricultural equipment and similar exhibits a dock becomes a necessity. It may, however, also require an observation point for communications equipment and door controls.

STORAGE

Storage requirements in the exhibition hall normally fall into two major categories: those of hall management and those of the exhibitors or show manager. Consideration of the first is absolutely necessary to the proper functioning of the facility and to maintaining reasonable operating costs. The second category of storage capabilities may prove to be elective.

Exhibit hall management requires space to store tables, chairs, material-handling equipment, platforms, and other items not in use during exhibitions.

Additional storage, possibly of a temporary nature, may be required by the decorator for items not currently in use by exhibitors.

Show management is faced with the need for crate and box storage for exhibitors during a show. Although on-site storage is highly desirable, in many cities show management is required to secure an off-site location. The additional handling and storage costs are then passed along to the exhibitors. When on-site storage is available, this accommodation should present a savings and could conceivably become a sales or marketing point for the building.

Another secondary advantage to providing on-site storage is that the move-out process would normally be accelerated and thus more rentable days would be realized for the facility. Interviews with drayage firms indicate that no standard volume of crate storage, adequate for all shows, has ever been set. The most reasonable ratio appears to be approximately 1 foot of storage for every 10 feet of net exhibition space used.

In lieu of permanent on-site storage, it is common practice, when sufficient exhibit space is available, to plan the booth layout to allow dead space to be set aside for crate storage. These areas are then draped off and hidden from public view by the decorator.

For exhibitions that generate a large volume of cardboard cartons drayage firms often prefer to place such highly flammable items in large vans outside the facility to reduce the fire hazard and the liability that would result.

RESTROOMS

Restrooms in an exhibition hall may require special consideration because exhibitors can be expected to use them as "employee washrooms." If space permits, separate dressing rooms are desirable. The installation of a laundry sink, plus hose bibs, at some convenient location is also recommended for use by exhibitors who have special cleaning or maintenance problems.

As an aid to admissions control and security requirements, sufficient restrooms should be located within control perimeters.

SECURITY

The security of the exhibits is a special concern. The concentration of emergency exits and other doorways, whenever possible, is essential, for it reduces guard service. Use of glass in security exits is not recommended.

Some of the larger exhibition halls have developed rather sophisticated television monitoring systems to improve security and reduce trade-show losses. Others employ electronic or mechanical alarm systems on exit doors and similar systems are installed for fire detection.

OFFICE SPACE

Major office space for administrative personnel is usually centrally located or accessible to all areas of the property, but at least minor on-site office space should be provided in the exhibition hall.

Show management also requires office space. In some cases it is located above the exhibit floor to provide an overview of the activity.

A first aid room, either in or immediately adjacent to the exhibit hall, is also called for.

PUBLIC ACCESS

When the exhibition hall serves as a convention site, normal requirements include a registration area and possibly a lounge area for delegates. In cities in which hotel accommodations are fragmented, the convention hall often serves as a gathering point.

The registration area should be located close to the main entrance of the hall and as near the exhibit area as possible. Although some trade shows prefer to register delegates inside the hall, most officials find it more convenient to locate this activity outside the exhibit area for the purpose of better control.

Registration counters are normally supplied by the show decorator, but ample power outlets for typewriters and other office equipment must be part of the permanent installation.

Some convention groups are now employing closed-circuit television systems as message indicators for their delegates. This would suggest the programming of adequate conduits for cables in the registration area and elsewhere in the hall.

When an exhibit hall is occupied by a consumer show open to the public, at least two ticket booths should be located under cover for protection from inclement weather.

Examples of exhibition halls are shown in Figures 37 to 42.

Figure 37. McCormick Place in Chicago, the world's largest exposition center, offers 2.5 million suqare feet of varied facilities for conventions and industrial exhibits. Located on the shores of Lake Michigan, McCormick Place has 700,000 square feet of exhibit space on two levels.

Figure 38. Constructed as part of the facilities for Hemisfair in 1968, the San Antonio Convention Center combines a large exhibition hall of more than 100,000 square feet plus an arena, theater, and many meeting rooms. The 750-foot Tower of the Americas is seen in the background. (Zintgraff Photographers.)

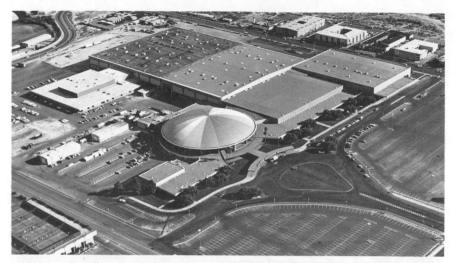

Figure 39. One of the larger exhibition halls in the United States is the Las Vegas Convention Center. Opened in 1959 with approximately 100,000 square feet of exhibition space, the complex has been expanded to nearly 500,000 square feet. Additional meeting rooms have also been constructed. (Las Vegas News Bureau.)

Figure 40. Flower and garden shows as well as plant shows are large users of exhibition space. Show producers often spend substantial sums for special features such as "waterfalls," "volcanos," or some equally unusual attraction.

74

Figure 41. Perhaps the most demanding exhibits in relation to ceiling heights are boat shows that feature sailing craft. When an arena adjoins or is close to the exhibition hall, these sailboats are often displayed in that space.

Figure 42. Aircraft of various types are almost dwarfed on display in an exhibit at one of the Las Vegas Convention Center exhibition halls. This particular show presents an interesting combination of salon space as seen in the foreground and the more conventional exhibit booths in the background. (Las Vegas News Bureau.)

9. Stadiums

Convinced that identity with "big league" teams means "big league" status, cities throughout North America have competed in recent years to make stadiums "the biggest game in town."

Not since the introduction of large university "bowls" and professional baseball fields in the early twenties and thirties has such a construction boom been witnessed. Perhaps none has ever equaled the monumental impact—good or bad—on their communities.

The ubiquitous monument of urban America in the Seventies is the sports stadium.

Civic pride can carry a high price tag, however, when expressed in concrete and steel. A relatively modest stadium can cost upwards of $30 million—and then fail to make enough money to pay for itself. Most, therefore, are financed with bonds issued by state, county or city governments that are supposed to be paid off by revenues derived from the project. But, in practice, these revenue bonds almost always turn out to load an open-ended general obligation on the taxpayer. Charles G. Burck, *Fortune* (March 1973).

Charles Maher of the Los Angeles Times summed up the situation:

"If you are going to build a major sports stadium today, you start out by digging a hole. That is where you are going to put the stadium. And that is probably where the stadium is going to put you."

Going back a few centuries, one of the first known stadiums was the foot race course at Olympia in ancient Greece. The term stadium, in fact, is derived from the Greek word *stadion* meaning "a measure of distance."

Other famous stadiums were located at Delphi, Athens, and Epidauras in Greece and Ephesus in Asia Minor. Terraces shaped like horseshoes on which seats were often built and which surrounded the field gave the spectators a clear view.

The Colosseum in Rome, built in A.D. 80, still stands as one of the world's great stadiums, and in 1896 the stadium at Athens was rebuilt for the Olympic games.

Today there are more than 1250 stadiums throughout the United States that seat 3000 or more. Estimated revenues are more than $300,000,000 annually, but because the typical number of days of use is only about 80 a year and because of the high costs of operation and a significant major bond indebtedness program, most modern-day facilities are a net financial load on their communities. Still, bigger and better stadiums are being built year after year.

Since 1965, when the Houston Astrodome was opened, hardly a year has gone by without the completion of another new stadium. Some seat 80,000 or more; others feature wall-to-wall artificial turf and have "exploding" scoreboards. A number provide exotic private suites for the wealthy or corporation executives, professional food and beverage services, and are more like modern hotels than yesterday's old ball parks.

As a result of this development, the meaning of "stadium," its functions and design, has become increasingly cloudy and difficult to define.

The "good old days" saw ball parks operated by the owners of major league teams and sometimes housing a newly formed professional football league as a second-rate tenant. Many of them, such as Comiskey Park, Wrigley Field, Fenway Park, Sportsman Park, and Ebbetts Field, to name only a few, were straightforward single-purpose structures.

The playing field was designed for baseball and if football could use it—fine. Seats were hard and narrow; many were merely boards. Restrooms were inadequate and concessions stands, crowded. Much of the seating area was devoted to bleacher sections and only a small portion was protected from the weather.

The playing fields of modern stadiums may be loosely grouped into three rather broad categories. Those designed for football or soccer, those designed for baseball, and those convertible to baseball, soccer, and football and a variety of other uses, including a track and field. Others, of course, are designed for highly specialized events such as swimming, tennis, and horse shows, but they represent only a small percentage of the total.

Regardless of the function, outdoor playing fields normally provide either "natural" or artificial turf. Much has been written on the virtues and economic considerations of both, but local conditions such as climate, soil, and volume of use dictate the ultimate decision.

Considerable interest has been expressed in many quarters regarding the potential of PAT (Prescription Athletic Turf), a system of underground utilities designed to water, drain, feed, and provide the correct temperatures needed for the fast and continuous growth of "natural" grass. Whether this system can produce a turf capable of sustaining heavy use over a period of time is still under observation.

Not unlike arenas, stadium seating has tended to offer ever-increasing comfort to spectators in the form of wider chairs, more individual seats, and more leg room. Development of high-impact plastics and molded seats has also done much to improve the esthetics of stadium seating. Bleacher seats can now be covered with aluminum or plastics, thus eliminating the danger of splintering and continual maintenance.

Adequate, modern, and conveniently located rest rooms also contribute their bit to spectator comfort.

Concessions, discussed in detail in Chapter 14, play a major role in stadiums—perhaps even more strongly than in arenas.

Multiple-use stadiums present unique problems for architects and engineers; for example, if the playing field is to be used for rock concerts or exhibitions (as proposed for some domed facilities), the designer is faced with the problem of spectator access to the playing field and also of providing concessions and adequate toilet facilities on field level. Utilities must also be supplied for exhibit use. These requirements are much the same as those discussed for exhibition halls in Chapter 8.

Private suites, discussed in Chapter 19, constitute another policy decision to be made in early design stages.

For facilities devoted to football and/or soccer, as well as track and field, a notable solution to the problem of crowd control and to the reduction of unwanted "sideliners" is found at Munich's Olympic Stadium, where a pit surrounds the field. This "dry moat" is provided as a gathering place for waiting athletes, coaches, and media photographers.

It is interesting to note that the line of demarcation between arena and stadium is becoming less distinctive year by year. Perhaps the time is approaching when only the total number of seats will determine when an arena becomes a domed stadium.

Some enthusiastic designers and engineers are contending that topless stadiums are a thing of the past and that long-span fabric roofs or air-support structures will be used in all future construction. Lower costs, improvement of products and techniques, and the capability of enclosing large areas for sports or entertainment purposes are all part of the new trend.

Many universities and government agencies are now considering the initiation of studies regarding the feasibility of covering their existing outdoor athletic facilities. Therefore there can be little doubt that the covered stadium is well on its way to becoming the new giant of the public assembly facility industry.

Figures 43 to 50 show several stadiums located throughout the United States.

Figure 43.   Host to the 1932 Olympics, the Los Angeles Coliseum has served the community well as a site for major league baseball, football, and many track and field events. Seating capacity is listed as 92,604.

Figure 44. One of the first examples of combining an outdoor stadium and an arena was the Oakland-Alameda County Coliseum Complex in California. The stadium at right seats 54,000 for major league sports. The arena contains 10,862 permanent seats. (Pacific Resources, Inc.)

Figure 45. Undoubtedly the most costly and perhaps the most controversial of the domed stadiums is the Louisiana Superdome. Constructed in the heart of New Orleans, the Superdome has 72,000 permanent seats.

Figure 46. Even a football field appears small when placed on the 166,000 square feet of the main hall of the Superdome. Built for baseball, as well as other sports, the height of the Superdome ceiling is listed as 280 feet.

Figure 47. A 1976 addition to the growing list of covered stadiums in the United States was the Kingdome in Seattle, Washington. Constructed by King County, the Kingdome contains 65,000 permanent seats. (Photo by Ted Larson.)

Figure 48. Pontiac Stadium is covered by what in 1977 was the world's largest air-supported roof. Located near Detroit, Michigan, the facility is the home of the Detroit Lions and has 80,400 seats at three levels.

Figure 49. Built at a reported cost of $38 million, the Astrodome opened in early 1965 as the world's first covered major league stadium. Located 6 miles from downtown Houston, Texas, the Astrodome has 45,000 seats for baseball and 52,000 for football. (Astrodome-Astrohall Stadium. Corporation.)

Figure 50. Constructed specifically for football, the interior of the Pontiac Stadium brings fans closer to the action on all sides of the playing field.

10. Meeting Rooms and Banquet Halls

Although meeting rooms, assembly rooms, and banquet halls are familiar features in most exhibition halls and convention centers, their requirements are nevertheless unique in many respects.

Of great interest has been the evolution of such areas from their initial utilitarian and sometimes sterile classroom appearance to today's highly finished, flexible installations that feature carpeted floors and upholstered seating (see Figures 51 and 52). Much of the change has undoubtedly been spurred by competition as cities, buildings, hotels and resorts vie for the lucrative convention, conference, and sales meeting market.

In some facilities one or more of their meeting rooms have become featured attractions in marketing the property and have added to their public image.

The most common flooring materials found in meeting rooms are proba-

Figure 51. Although most meeting rooms are constructed with flat floors for multipurpose use, this one at McCormick Place in Chicago provides permanent theater-type seating. The sloping floor supports 350 seats in each of the Little Theaters which offer almost unlimited opportunities for audiovisual presentations.

Figure 52. A typical meeting room with chairs in "auditorium" style set approximately 32 inches back-to-back and ganged together in accordance with local fire codes. A head table and floor lectern complete the arrangements. (Photograph by Ackroyd Photography, Inc.)

bly vinyl asbestos tile and hardwood, although carpeting is fast becoming a favorite. Not only does carpeting add to the acoustical properties of the space, it also provides a general feeling of luxury. Another factor favoring the use of carpeting is its lower maintenance cost compared with other types of floor covering.

Some operators, when faced with multiple-use problems, have opted for concrete floors with removable carpeting—taking up the carpeting for exhibit-type events or those activities for which carpeting would not be desirable. Still others, whose carpeting is permanently installed, rely on portable hardwood dance floors for temporary installation.

Walls present a major maintenance problem in meeting rooms. Acoustics are important, and esthetics must be considered. Still, posters, signs, and bulletins with their ever-present adhesive tape remain a constant threat to all types of finish. Fortunately many products capable of withstanding the rigors of tape, tacks, and scraping are now available.

Careful choice of equipment such as chairs with "wall-saver" legs can also help to reduce damage. Tack strips and hanging devices can do their bit. Many meeting rooms employ some form of wainscoting to help protect the finishes.

Many planners recommend ceiling heights of not less than 15 feet. The primary reason for higher ceilings is that the stage or head-table riser in many rooms elevates the speakers or performers far too close to a standard 8- or 10-foot ceiling for comfort or safety. Of equal importance is the need for a ceiling of sufficient height to permit the projection of motion pictures and slide films on a large-scale screen (see Figure 53).

Acoustical requirements in both walls and ceilings of most meeting rooms can generally be described as those best for the spoken word, for their function is generally focused on verbal rather than musical activities.

Of equal or perhaps even greater importance in considering the acceptability of meeting rooms is the soundproofing of these areas. This requirement often introduces the need for careful, and probably costly, designs when flexible or adjustable spaces created by movable wall panels are programmed.

Few public buildings experience greater exposure to embarrassing situation than those in which a religious meeting can easily find itself scheduled near—if not adjacent to—a high school dance featuring the town's most enthusiastic rock musicians. Extreme attention must be given to the development of proper specifications and "client understanding" of the various types and qualities of room separators or dividers. Some products work well; others provide little more than visual separation. For good sound isolation purposes the mechanical features of the room must be properly designed if any portable wall is to function adequately.

Figure 53. Flat-floor meeting rooms require ceiling heights of 15 feet or more if they are to serve the audiovisual needs of their users. In this typical meeting room setup the speakers platform is elevated approximately 24 inches above the floor.

Although perhaps esthetically pleasing, the need for windows in meeting rooms is generally negative. Not only can windows distract those who attend the meetings, they also require "blackout" draperies when motion pictures or slides are to be shown. In short, meetings rarely *need* windows. Disadvantages are multiple—benefits few.

Depending on the size of each meeting room, sound amplification may or may not be required. When deemed desirable, this matter must be addressed in a manner that will give each meeting space individual and easily operated controls.

Each meeting room should be equipped with a "house telephone" or intercommunications system that will enable the lessee to call for a custodian or events supervisor when needed.

Meeting-room illumination is highly important and must be sufficiently flexible to meet the changing uses and demands of the space. Obviously the light-level requirements of a sales meeting will vary substantially from those of a dinner party of dance. Dimmers as well as "black-out" switches must be provided to accommodate film presentations.

Perhaps one of the most difficult and debatable topics concerning meeting rooms is that of number and size. The requirements vary from user to user to such an extent that only flexible spaces can present the ultimate answer. Generally speaking, there appears to be great need among most associations and other groups for small assemblies. Whether called seminars, workshops, group encounters, or team discussions, the demand is the same. Meeting planners today believe that for many reasons the major unit of delegates should be divided into smaller segments. Because this concept is not expected to change in the foreseeable future, facilities management must be prepared to respond to it if they expect to attract business.

Most discussion has been directed to the use of meeting rooms for business purposes. Of perhaps equal importance and volume in many locations are social functions, such as banquets (See Figures 54 and 55).

Whether considering a mid-morning coffee break at a sales meeting or a full-scale dinner dance, the accommodations for food and beverage service must be carefully designed. The relation of each meeting room to the kitchen and/or servery should be given exact study, for it can mean the difference between profit and loss. In major facilities or complexes in which food and beverage service is to play a major role, employment of a qualified consultant to assist in the proper development of spacial relationships, quantification of areas, and specification of equipment is recommended.

The location of meeting rooms in a facility is important not only to the

Figure 54.   Tables for this large banquet, set in herringbone style, favor the large head table. At one end is a portable stage for special entertainment. A high wall of curtains blocks arena seats from the view of the diners. (Photograph by Photo-Art Studios.)

Figure 55. Banquet business is big business in most convention centers. This room in Chicago's McCormick Place can accommodate 1400 persons for lucheons or banquets. Removable carpeting is perhaps the most popular floor covering. Some operators, however, prefer permanent carpeting and use portable hardwood floors for dancing.

owner and/or manager who is seeking maximum utilization of the property but also to those persons interested in leasing the rooms; for example, meeting planners are quick to point out the advisability of locating meeting spaces as close as possible to exhibit halls or display areas. Local users wishing to lease single meeting rooms are interested in their ready accessibility and easy identification. Meeting rooms must also be near restrooms, vending machines, and public telephones. Management must locate these spaces within control perimeters and reasonably close to custodial rooms, storage spaces and other support features.

Finally, the display of large-scale equipment for product introductions, sales meetings, and similar functions indicates the need for a strong link between meeting rooms and loading docks. All rooms of any substantial size should be provided with at least one double door for the passage of automobiles or other large items.

Because of their extreme flexibility of function and purpose, meeting rooms provide a formidable challenge to planning, design, and location.

FUNCTION ROOM SETUPS

Function-room capacities are customarily estimated by dividing the total square footage by certain accepted space requirements; for example, 7 to 8 square feet per person are usually considered adequate for "auditorium-style" seating. In this arrangement chairs are placed in rows approximately 36 to 42 inches apart and divided by a center aisle and all face the stage or speaker's platform.

For food functions most operators recommend 10 square feet per person when rectangular tables are placed end to end and around 12 square feet per person when round tables are used.

"School-room style" setups, in which all persons are seated at rectangular tables facing in one direction, require additional square footage, depending on the width of the tables.

Room capacities are often overestimated when sufficient space has not been deducted from available totals for a stage, platform, head table, or food-serving area.

Correct planning and development of function rooms can be greatly improved by sketching various setups in the proposed areas to determine whether the space can, in fact, accommodate the desired numbers under a wide variety of seating arrangements. Some typical setups are shown in Figures 56 to 59.

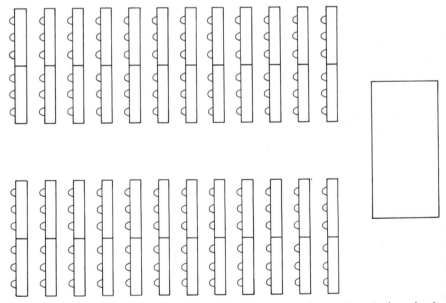

Figure 56. Schoolroom Style. One acceptable arrangement for meetings is the schoolroom or classroom style in which attendees are seated at tables facing in the same direction. Standard rectangular banquet tables may be used, but a special table 18 inches wide saves space. This arrangement is endorsed by meeting planners, in particular when delegates are expected to take notes.

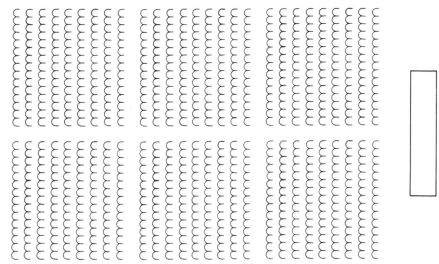

Figure 57.   Function Room Setups. The variety of functions and setups for meeting rooms is unlimited. Flexibility of use and the versatility of the spaces involved are of utmost importance in their design. Certain arrangements, however, have become somewhat basic to the industry. Perhaps the most familiar of all meeting room setups is the auditorium style. In this arrangement all chairs face the stage, speakers platform, or podium. Rows are spaced in accordance with local fire codes.

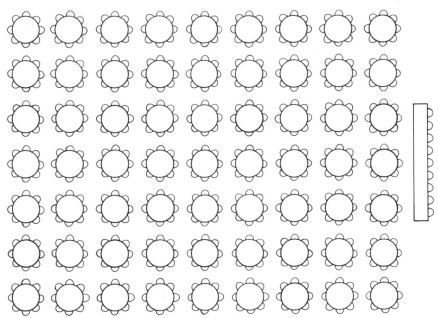

Figure 58.   Round Tables—Highly favored by most planners for food functions is the round table seating 8 or 10 persons. In this arrangement all diners face inward creating a more intimate conversational atmosphere. Spacing of tables and chairs is of great importance in providing proper circulation for both guests and food-handling personnel as well.

Figure 59. **Perpendicular Schoolroom Style.** A variation of the classic "schoolroom style" shown in Figure 56. This arrangement is used when space is at a premium and by facilities unable to provide the narrow schoolroom-type tables. Delegates have use of the tables for note taking but face the speakers rostrum at an angle. It is also a familiar banquet setup for a limited space or when banquet rounds are not available.

11. Equipment

Proper selection of equipment is a key to the success of any audience support facility. All too often, however, the inventory to be acquired and an adequate budget for its purchase fail to be given serious thought until at last the task must be completed in a hasty and disorganized manner.

From such delays come compromises in design, function, and quality that may well affect the operational capabilities of the building for many years to come.

Responsibility for the selection and specification of equipment often falls to the architect and his professional staff. In some cases it is given to the contractor as part of his overall bid. In still others the acquisition of many items is left to government purchasing agents and sometimes to inexperienced managers.

The construction of a public assembly facility is often a first-time experience for many government jurisdictions; elected officials or appointed members of commissions rarely possess the knowledge or expertise to select those items that will best serve the long-term needs of the building, its staff, and lessees.

Ideally, the architect should be fully aware of the equipment that will be required and how it will affect design. Advance agreement should exist between the owner and the architect regarding the items of equipment to be specified and selected by the architect, those to be obtained by the owner, and those by the manager and his staff.

Many factors, not the least of which can be government purchasing regulations, must be considered. Some "owners" believe that a lower fee from the architect can be developed if he is restricted from participating in the specification of equipment. Others take the attitude that elected officials should place their stamp of approval or rejection on all "large-ticket" items. Regardless of the reasoning, the fact remains that the hundreds of thousands of dollars to be spent for equipment should be expended for the best possible products for the purpose intended.

The need is clear for the development of an early understanding between the architect, purchasing agent, legal counsel, and government administration. This understanding should indicate well in advance how the equipment is to be funded, who will be responsible for its specification and purchase, the timetable for purchase and delivery, and who will be in charge of coordinating the entire package.

Excellent results have often been achieved by the specification of major items by the architect working with the guidance of a professional consultant or experienced facility manager. Under this plan the architect is responsible for such equipment items as permanent seating, telescoping risers, hockey-rink dashers, portable seating, corridor and lobby furniture, and portable basketball floors.

Not only does this program allow the architect to control the physical coordination of equipment with structure, but it also helps him to develop his basic design theme.

In theater design the architect is generally assisted by a theater consultant and an acoustician; between them they develop plans and specifications for stage equipment, sound reinforcement, concert shell, and other special or technical items.

For arenas, exhibition halls, and multipurpose facilities more generalized items such as lift trucks, ice resurfacing machines, floor scrubbers, and shop equipment can be made the responsibility of a purchasing agent working under the supervision and assistance of a consultant or manager.

Finally, the myriad last-minute small items and operating supplies can be specified and purchased by the manager and his staff as the date for the facility opening nears.

Once the equipment has been received, preventive maintenance should be implemented from the day it is first placed in use. Little question exists that such a program can easily double the life of most items.

INVENTORY

Development of an inventory is perhaps as individualized and specialized as the facility itself. Although some items may have a function in both sports arena and concert hall, many have not. Some items common to the public assembly field are the following:

Attraction Boards

These items may be called attraction boards, announcement boards, marque boards, or whatever, but their function is the same—to inform the public of current and/or upcoming events. In most new facilities these boards are free standing and are located at a point or points of high-count street traffic.

Most economical and still perhaps the most common are the change-letter type with plastic letters hung on the face of an illuminated background. Gaining in popularity, however, are electronic or computerized message centers that permit a great variety of displays in electric lights or reflective disks. By employing computer or punch-tape devices messages or announcements may be changed at will merely by typing the information into a console located inside the facility. The board can also be programmed to add or remove certain messages automatically.

Benches

Benches, both fixed and portable, are used in dressing rooms, sports events and corridors for seating performers, athletes, and patrons. Depending on their use and purpose, they may be wooden, metal, plastic, upholstered, or any combination of these materials.

Beds

Either hospital beds or examination tables are customarily found in public assembly facility first-aid rooms.

Basketball Floors

Because most arenas have concrete floors, portable, hardwood basketball floors are needed. These floors come in sections locked together by special fastening devices (see Figures 60 and 61).

Basketball Goals

Single-post, roll-away basketball goals that feature glass backboards are the current favorite of most professional and collegiate teams. Replacements for these glass backstops should also be provided and spare basket rings are needed, as is a supply of nets.

Carpeting

Carpeting, both removable and permanently installed, is becoming more popular and practical in many areas of public assembly facilities.

Control Hardware

Although roll-down or collapsible gates may be categorized as control hardware, the equipment under consideration here includes portable stan-

Figure 60. Almost without exception modern arenas are constructed with concrete floors that call for the use of portable hardwood basketball courts. This flooring is customarily built in panels approximately 4' x 8' with special locking devices. Trained workmen can lay or remove a floors in an extremely short time. (Championship Sports Floors, Inc.)

Figure 61.   Both basketball floor panels and ice covers are customarily stored on steel trucks. To conserve storage space most storage trucks are constructed for hoisting by fork lifts and are stacked two or three high. (Championship Sports Floors, Inc.)

dards, fences, stancheons, ropes, and other items normally used to indicate closed areas, places for patrons to queue, and perhaps directional guides.

Standards are often chrome or brushed aluminum and may have heavy bases or be screwed into floor sockets. Ropes are plasticized or fabric-covered. For larger spaces or when more positive control is required portable fencing built on heavy bases or rollers is used.

Coat Racks

Depending on the space available and climatic conditions, coat and hat racks may be permanent or portable. Equipment is much the same except that portable equipment is usually wheel-mounted or folding.

Cleaners (vacuum)

Most facilities must have one or more industrial vacuum cleaners capable of sweeping a wide path and with sufficient power to pick up cups, paper, and other trash. Still larger cleaners will be required if the facility maintains its own parking lots and other outdoor areas. Smaller vacuums are needed for carpeting in meeting rooms, offices, and other spaces.

Floor Scrubbers

Industrial floor scrubbers are "must" items for arenas and exhibition halls. Their use in smaller facilities depends on the area of hard-finish floors to be maintained.

Flags and Flag Poles

In the design of exterior flag poles care must be taken to protect the halyard or whatever mechanism is employed for raising and lowering the flag from vandalism.

Sports arenas require the prominent display of the national flag. Facilities should be provided as well for at least one other flag required when teams or performers from another country are featured. Some dramatic lighting of the flags is also desirable.

Smaller interior flags with poles and floor bases are displayed in meeting rooms, at head tables, and on speaker's platforms. Flags of many countries are sometimes needed for international gatherings, and many publicly owned facilities also display state, county, or city flags.

Arenas that house professional teams may also fly league pennants, banners, or heralds on a permanent basis. Provision for displaying these flags plus the capability of removing them for cleaning should be made.

Fire Extinguishers

Requirements for fire extinguishers are spelled out in most building codes. Some problems, however, are unique to public assembly facilities; for example, in crowded corridors it is difficult to see the extinguishers if they are placed too low on the walls. Special precautions must be taken to protect these devices from theft, vandalism, or pranksters, and in exhibition halls special attention must be paid to their location so that their placement will not prove disruptive to a practical arrangement of display booths.

First Aid Room

Movable equipment will include one or more hospital beds or examination tables, pillows, and linens. Screens if not affixed will be portable. Other items are a small desk or table for the attendant plus a comfortable chair, side chairs or stools for each bed, a medicine chest with a lock, fold-up wheelchairs, fold-up stretchers; resuscitation equipment, and pans and other hospital ware.

Garden Tools

Depending on the amount and type of landscaping, necessary garden tools include a lawn mower, shovels, rakes, and hoses.

Hand Trucks

Hand trucks and perhaps a hydraulic-lift dolly may be useful and/or required, depending on the facility.

Identification Equipment

Various methods of equipment labeling or identification are required, and all items should be affixed with an identifying mark and/or number. Some common systems employ stencils, electric branding irons, decals, or an electric styllus.

Mirrors

Fixed mirrors in restrooms and dressing rooms are items specified in the construction contract. Arenas that cater to ice shows, circuses, and other touring attractions with large casts will need portable mirrors for use when temporary dressing rooms are required.

Microphones

Sound reinforcement equipment may also be listed in the construction contract or specified in a separate document developed by the acoustician or some other specialist. In either event a large number and variety of microphones will be required.

Matting

Safety matting or runners for entries and other areas during inclement weather must be supplied.

Padlocks

Padlocks, master-keyed and with chains or cables encased in plastic, are used in quantity. When permitted by fire regulations, these are simple devices designed to secure exits equipped with panic hardware.

Lecterns

Lecterns of two heights are commonly used: one for table tops, the other free standing. Lighting and receptacles for mounting microphones are affixed on lecterns.

Platforms

Elevated platforms are required to serve as portable stages, banquet risers, and runways used for fashion shows (see Figure 62). Three different systems of installing elevated platforms are common. One employs "construction-type" supports, joined to provide a sturdy base on which plywood plates are placed to form a stage floor. This type is extremely flexible for expansion is easy. Its initial cost is perhaps the lowest and it probably requires the least amount of storage space but its set up is the most expensive.

A second type features folding legs attached to a heavy-duty top similar to a folding table. Each section is affixed to another to form a solid platform of whatever size is required. More expensive than the first type, folding-leg platforms nevertheless store compactly, and erection time and labor required are substantially less.

The third and most sophisticated form has all supporting members permanently attached to the platform. The entire section moves on its own casters and when located is designed to secure all legs and braces automatically and at the same time raise the wheels into a resting position. It is, however, the most expensive insofar as capital cost is concerned. It needs the greatest amount of storage space but the least amount of labor, for no lift-trucks or other handling equipment are necessary.

Paint Sprayer

A paint sprayer, rollers, brushes, and other similar items must be supplied for normal maintenance work.

Risers

Perhaps the most common is the aluminum telescoping riser that employs fixed fold-down seats or portable folding chairs. This equipment demands close coordination between fixed and temporary seating areas. Aisles and slightlines must be considered.

Whenever possible, telescoping risers are permanently affixed to the structure. Often, however, they are designed to be entirely removable from the arena floor. Most are designed to provide maximum seating capacities

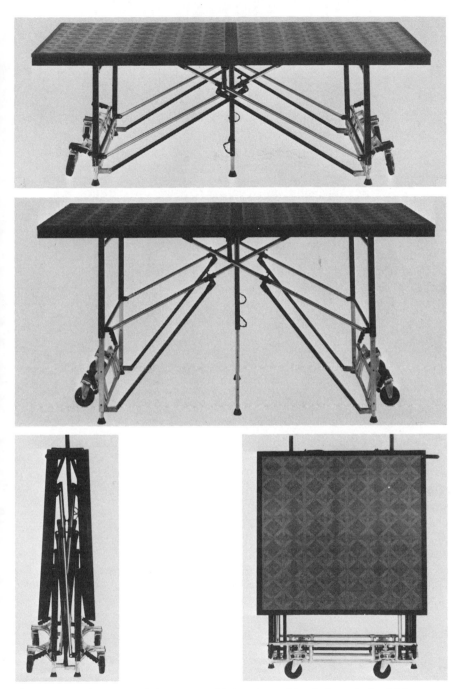

Figure 62. Perhaps one of the most sophisticated portable platforms is the folding stage shown here. This particular model offers varying heights, has attached wheels for rolling into storage, and can be erected or dismantled by one man. (Sico, Inc.)

for basketball and are then telescoped to give the additional floor space needed for hockey without dismantling the entire assembly.

An inherent problem in the development of temporary or portable seating is that it often occupies a choice location. Tickets for these seats may easily be the most expensive in the house, thus making visability and comfort top priority matters.

Saws

Portable electric, radial arm, and a variety of hand saws must be obtained.

Seating

The subject of fixed and portable seating in all types of audience support facilities is complicated at best. The matter is discussed in a special subsection devoted to the many choices available.

Storage Cabinets

Whether built-in or free-standing, all departments require cabinets with strong locks for the secure storage of hand tools, supplies, and other equipment.

Show Card Holders

To avoid indiscriminate posting of announcements in arenas and other facilities, it is desirable to provide permanently affixed show card holders.

Spotlights

High-intensity follow-spotlights located in high-level baskets or platforms are required in all arenas. They are also standard equipment in theaters. Some models have proved to be noisy and may require special housing or other consideration. Placement of the platforms must be closely coordinated with the physical capabilities of the lights if they are to cover all areas of the arena floor properly.

Other smaller follow-spots are customarily used in assembly and banquet halls. A variety of *fixed* spotlights and floodlights is another requirement.

Tools

All facilities must have a substantial inventory of hand tools plus necessary storage chests.

Ticket Racks

If standard printed reserved seat tickets are to be used, ticket racks are essential. Racks are normally wall-mounted with removable interior sections.

Ticket Boxes

Ticket boxes or receptacles are a standard item in all facilities. They are usually provided with a removable inner container of cloth, metal, or wood.

Turnstiles

Turnstiles are designed to provide an accurate mechanical accounting of attendance totals. They come in two basic styles: portable models that are mounted on heavy steel bases (Figure 62) or permanent models that are bolted to the floor (Figure 63).

Tables

A wide choice of tables, depending on the functions and need of the facility must be made:

Work tables will be needed for offices, work shops, and kitchens.

Rectangular folding tables are approximately 30 inches high. Most are 30 inches wide and come in 4-, 6-, and 8-foot lengths: 6-foot tables are used for head tables, U-shaped arrangements, board of director's setups, buffets, registrations, and displays; 8-foot and 4-foot tables are used with the 6-foot tables to adjust the setup to the size of the room and the number of people to be seated; 6-foot tables, 18 inches wide, are normally used for "schoolroom style" setups to preserve space.

Rectangular stacking tables are now offered by at least one manufacturer in both 4- and 6-foot lengths.

Round folding tables are approximately 30 inches high: 4-foot round tables are useful as cocktail tables for receptions; 60-inch round tables seat 8 to 10 persons and 72-inch round tables seat 10 to 12. Specialty folding tables include half-rounds, quarter-rounds, and serpentines used for the construction of special setups for food displays and buffets.

Projector tables are highly recommended in a 42-inch height for projectors. They should be mounted on casters and equipped with extension cords at least 25 feet long. A four-outlet box is normally affixed under the top surface

Figure 63.   An important item of admissions control equipment is the turnstile, whether temporary or permanent. This particular model is equipped with wheels to permit easy handling and quick removal. (Perey Turnstiles.)

of these tables to provide power for the slide projector, a film projector, a small reading light, and possibly an electric pointer.

Towel Dispensers

A variety of options is available in restroom fixtures such as towel dispensers. This equipment may be part of the construction contract but the final decision regarding paper towels versus electric hand dryers should be made only after consultation with a facility consultant or experienced manager.

Figure 64. Close attention must be given to the design of admissions control. Shown here are fixed guide railings, turnstiles, and ticket boxes. In this example, the gateman stands to the side of the turnstile. By merely leaning against a lock on the side of the turnstile, he can block the entrance of a patron. (Perey Turnstiles)

Urns

Some type of sand urn or ash stand for cigarette butts and other burning material is necessary.

Waste Receptacles

Waste or trash receptacles are obtainable in a wide range of sizes, shapes, and colors. For more sophisticated facilities it may be desirable to design special equipment. The primary concern is that the receptacles be easy to empty and large enough for any specific event without requiring service at midpoint. It is also interesting to note that receptacles that do not require touching to open are customarily better used.

Work Benches

Work benches, attached vices, and other shop equipment are needed.

Window-cleaning Equipment

Window-cleaning equipment will depend entirely on facility design.

Vehicles

Vehicular equipment for arenas usually includes two or more forklift trucks, electric carts, and possibly a pick-up truck.

EQUIPMENT FOR AN ICE RINK

Hockey Dashers

Most hockey dashers are manufactured by national concerns, but some are built locally. Of primary importance in arenas with many schedule changes is ease of installation and removal. Also a vital part of planning and coordination is the placement of the necessary floor inserts to anchor supports for the dashers.

Because of normal wear and tear, provisions must be made for the replacement of kick boards and other sections. Dashers are normally placed on wheeled dollies or carts and remain there while in storage. These carts must be purchased or built at the same time as the dashers.

Hockey Screens

Almost all modern arenas now employ glass screens, although wire fencing is still in use. These glass sections are normally made of plexiglass or a special tempered material and are held in place by special metal frames from which they are removed for storage. Special wheeled dollies with protective padding are used to handle the glass sections. The storage carts are purchased at the same time as the screens and are designed with racks divided to fit them.

Hockey Goals

At least one set of goals, plus a spare, is required for ice hockey. Included in the equipment inventory are nets for the goals plus one or more spares. Included with the hockey goals are the goal lights. Electric conduits for connecting the lights to the time clock and other scoring mechanisms should be installed in the floor.

Ice Rink Covers

Covers for the ice sheet are provided by several different methods. The two most common are panels of marine plywood mounted on 2 x 4 stringers or panels of special "sandwich" board (two sides of plywood and a central core of lightweight insulation material). Rink covers customarily consist of 4 x 8 foot panels and certain sections cut to accommodate the curved radii of the rink. Some commercial versions of rink covers are on the market.

Ice Paint Mixers

Because most ice paints are water soluble and require special handling, frequent mixing is necessary. This equipment is designed to stir the paint continuously and then pump it under pressure for spraying.

Ice Removal Equipment

A variety of systems is employed to remove ice from the arena floor. Equipment inventories commonly call for some type of tractor capable of operating on an ice surface, plus the necessary attachments to "plow" and break up the ice and then push the chunks into a pit or out of the building.

Ice Resurfacer

So dominant in the field is the "Zamboni" that the name has become synonymous with ice resurfacing equipment. Its inventor, Frank Zamboni, was a pioneer in the development of the first mechanical means of resurfacing (see Figure 65). This machine is designed to shave the surface of the ice to remove rough spots and blade grooves. The shavings, or "snow," are automatically lifted into the resurfacer. It then deposits a sheet of hot water over the surface which is further smoothed by a cloth squeegee to leave a nearly perfect finish almost instantly.

Figure 65. Invented by Frank Zamboni of Paramount, California, this ice resurfacing machine is designed to shave the surface of the ice, remove the "snow," and at the same time spray hot water to give an almost instant flat surface. Before the arrival of the "Zamboni" on the scene, these operations were performed by hand.

Here are a few more items.

Audiovisual Equipment

Whether a facility provides a wide variety of audiovisual equipment or requires the lessee to rent it commercially appears to be a local decision. Rapidly changing conditions, however, make its inclusion in inventory, as well as its scope, a subject for careful consideration.

Boxing Ring

An arena may be required to provide a boxing ring. (Wrestling rings are smaller and are customarily supplied by the commercial promoter.) In addition, the inventory must contain corner posts, ropes, ring cover, padding, steps, corner stools, and ring lights.

Chalkboards

Fixed boards are standard items in dressing rooms and other locations. Portable chalkboards are needed for meeting rooms.

Easels

Folding easels are required for meeting rooms.

Employee Lockers

Lockers in which employees can leave clothing or valuables while at work must be provided.

Organ

Most arenas are equipped with an electric organ. Its size and quality will probably depend on the budget.

Pianos

Small upright pianos and benches equipped with protective covers are needed in most facilities. The number will depend on the building's size and schedule. Theaters and concert halls normally provide at least one grand piano as part of standard inventory.

Picture Screens

A large commercial screen may be needed if the facility is programmed to present closed-circuit television attractions, and at least one small portable screen is desirable as part of a convention center inventory. Special screens, particularly in large number, are rented.

Track and Field Equipment

Arenas that promote indoor track and field events will need portable tracks for both distance and dashes (Figure 66) as well as specialized equipment for field activities (Figure 67).

Office Equipment

The following items represent a general outline of basic office equipment:

- Adding machines and calculators
- Addressing machine
- Bookcases
- Card files
- Clocks
- Conference room chairs
- Copying machine

Figure 66. Indoor track and field meets have become regular features in many arenas throughout the United States. Portable equipment consists of a circular track for distance events, straight-away for dashes and hurdles, and runways for both the pole vault and broad jump. (Championship Sports Floors, Inc.)

Figure 67. The "convertible" stadium, which calls for frequent removal of artificial turf, brought about the creation of a new member of the "Zamboni" family, the "Grasshopper." This unusual machine lays down and picks up rolls of Astro-turf (R) 15 feet wide, 5 feet in diameter and weighing approximately 3000 pounds. The "Grasshopper" places the rolls of "carpeting" on specially designed racks for storage.

- Desks
- Desk chairs, executive
- Desk chairs, secretarial
- Dictation equipment
- Duplicating equipment
- File cabinets
- Punches
- Safe
- Side chairs
- Staplers
- Storage cabinets
- Typewriters
- Wastebaskets

SEATING

In most public assembly facilities seating is divided into two rather general categories: fixed and portable. From that point on the choice, particularly of movable equipment, is a broad one.

Permanent or fixed seating is exactly that. The chairs are bolted to the floor or to the risers to remain for years of service. Obviously quality and durability must be stressed if they are to provide such long service.

Because this seating cannot be moved, sightlines for all types of event for which the facility will be used must be carefully studied in the design of the seating areas.

Engineers for the American Seating Company have summarized their views on the subject of arena design:

During the past 15 years there has been a tremendous program of construction of arena-type buildings throughout the United States and in some foreign countries. There have been new buildings of capacities varying from 3,000 seats through the 10,000 to 20,000 seat range and into the very large structures like the Astrodome, Kingdome and Superdome.

With this wide variation in sizes and capacities it is impossible to establish and recommend any specific design and layout to be the best answer to accommodating the patron and providing each one with the best seat in the house. We can, however, establish a few criteria and parameters that will facilitate movement into and out of the seating areas and provide the patron with comfortable seating space and a good view of what he has paid to see.

In all areas of the country there are local, state or national building codes that must be studied and met by any proposed construction. Areas or localities that will not permit more than 14 chairs between aisles, as an example, will certainly require a different arrangement of those aisles in comparison with an area that may allow as many as 20 or more chairs between them; and, particularly so, if in both areas we are trying to design for the same seating capacity. The building with the tighter restriction on chairs between aisles may require another 5 percent in added chair rows to provide the same number of seats around the same size of arena floor.

A symmetrical arrangement of centralized aisles and exits is quite fundamental in utilizing as much of the area of seating decks as possible for the placement of chairs. Diagram 1 (Figure 68) shows the use of aisles centered on the exits. This necessitates more exits and aisle space and can result in congestion in the flow of traffic at the exits. While this arrangement eliminates the need for any cross aisle (depending on building code requirements), it requires an exit to be located at every aisle.

A better arrangement of aisles and requiring fewer exits is shown in Diagram 2 (Figure 69). In this plan the exits are located in every other bank of chairs and open into a cross aisle. The longitudinal aisles forward of the cross aisle are centered on the exits and on the full chair bank between exits. In this arrangement a wider cross aisle is substituted for one row of chairs and the center exit shown in Diagram 1. With only a slight decrease in capacity for similar lengths of chair rows, the arrangement shown in Diagram 2 provides better traffic flow in and out of the seating areas.

The layout of Diagram 2 is satisfactory for areas having low platforms. A problem is created however, in balconies or platform areas having high risers. To overcome sightline difficulties for the rows behind the cross aisle, it usually is necessary to increase the elevation of all of these rows. This can be achieved by expansion of the vomitory (exit) width to provide stairs to the upper areas, as shown in Diagram 3 (Figure 70). Here, again, the traffic flow is excellent and direction of the patrons for both the upper and lower areas can be controlled by the ushers at the rear of the exits.

The design of the chair platforms for depth of tread and height of risers has been given considerable attention. Building codes for many areas specify the minimum depth of platforms and maximum height of risers that may be used. These require-

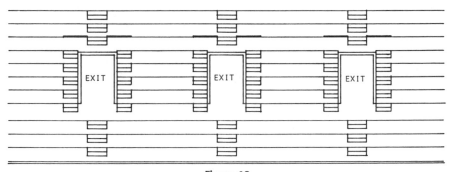

Figure 68.

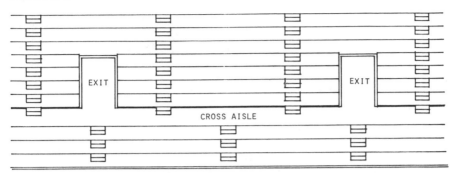

Figure 69.

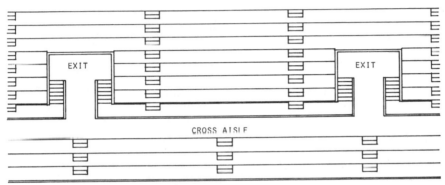

Figure 70.

ments must be given first consideration. The second factor to consider then in this design relates to the activities that are to be viewed by the patrons.

In recent years several buildings have been planned and built to accommodate both hockey and basketball teams. Because of the variation in size of the standard playing areas required for these two sports, some compromise usually is required in the establishment of the floor area that is to be seen from all seats. This minimum vision area is referred to as the focal point or focal point perimeter. If we design all rows to have good, clear vision to the dasher or to a line on the ice near the dasher, then it would be reasonable to assume that there is even better vision to the sides or ends of the basketball court. This is generally true. Because of the fact that the end of the basketball floor is about 45 feet away from the end of the hockey dasher, however, it means that the front row of end zone seats for basketball is also that far away from the action. If loose seats are to be placed on the arena floor to utilize this open area, we encounter a problem immediately with seeing the action on the basketball floor. If the seats on the floor are placed on elevated platforms, those patrons will block the vision of the people behind the dashers at the ends, unless they are given enough elevation to see over them. If the rows behind the dasher are raised enough to provide this clear vision to the basketball area, then it is probably true that these same elevated front rows of seats will now block the vision of several rows of seats behind them for seeing hockey action in the near end zone.

It is imperative, therefore, in the design of any arena that all of these matters relating to the major design goals be discussed fully and that the various types of programs be weighed for relative importance to determine the design parameters. Any compromises with visual requirements should be understood by all involved in the design and utilization of the building. Full data should also be sought on types of equipment that may minimize vision problems and increase the flexibility of use of the building. Many of the new arenas now contain permanent or fixed seats in certain elevated areas with some of the lower rows of seats of the foldaway or removable types mounted on telescopic platforms. This combination of fixed and movable seating can also provide some of the answers to the sightline compromises that may be required between various types of sports or other performances. This can become a complicated design problem and manufacturers of such equipment should be consulted in the early design stages.

Once the design criteria have been established and visual goals are determined, the focal points or focal planes can then be set. With these criteria the heights of risers and platform depths can be worked out in sightline studies. In Diagram 4 (Figure 71) we show the elements of such a study. In this case we are assuming that there are telescopic or removable platforms for the lower six rows and fixed seating rows above them. (Note the overhang of the front rows of fixed seating platforms to accommodate the telescopic platforms in the closed configuration.) In this illustration we show an end-zone section of a hockey arena with the focal point located at the goal line and slightly above the ice level. In the rows shown we have established the riser heights needed with a previously determined platform (tread) depth to obtain 5 inches or more of sightline clearance on a two-row basis. By graphic layout

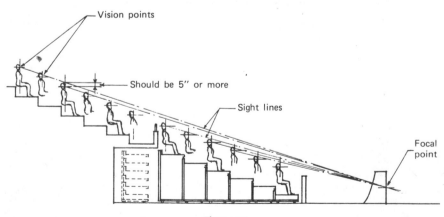

Figure 71.

or by mathematical calculations we can continue the study for more rows behind those shown and determine the riser heights needed for providing this minimum of 5 inches of clearances.

Many of the newer arenas have been built with precast concrete platforms. Each of these platforms provides a vertical riser face along with the horizontal tread surface. They are designed to be assembled on the supporting beam structures and achieve the configuration needed to give the established sightlines. Since the chairs are usually attached to the riser faces, to facilitate cleaning operations, it is critical that the riser portions be of sufficient strength and thickness (minimum of 4½ inches) and that the necessary reinforcing steel rods or cables be located to provide sufficient clear area and depth for installation of the anchors needed to hold the chairs.

Because of the continuing trend toward the increasing size of people, most of the newer structures are providing more knee room and hip room for the seated patrons. Minimum chair size in most buildings of recent years has been set at 19 inches in width, and a few have tried to hold to 20 inches. Likewise, minimum platform depths have shown a similar trend and we now find 34 inches to 36 inches being used for many projects. In upper areas, where risers must be made higher to provide proper sight lines, it will be found necessary to increase the platform depth to maintain adequate knee room and passing room through the chair rows. Again, some of the applicable building codes eatablish the minimum platform depths that can be used with various riser heights.

From the comments made here, it is clear that those responsible for the design of an arena must be thoroughly familiar with the details of the building code that applies in the locality. These codes are written to protect the patron by providing aisles of proper width and numbers, adequate seating areas, proper protection against falls, requirements for safety rails and sufficient illumination of aisles. Chair manufacturers are familiar with most code requirements and are prepared to provide and install equipment in full compliance with these requirements.

(The American Seating Company manufactures products for the education, amusement and transportation markets. It has provided the permanent seating for more major sports facilities than any other company.)

For safety and ease of sweeping, chairs with self-lifting seats are used in most modern arenas. The major decision, however, that will face the owner and architect will be whether to select fully or partly upholstered, plastic, or wooden chairs. Often budget inadequacy settles the issue quickly.

By far the majority of new arenas, however, have determined that the comfort of the patron overrides any temptation to economize on seating. Most have specified chairs with padded seats and backs, although some have opted for only cushioned seats. Few, if any, public auditoriums or theaters have been constructed in recent years without the installation of fully upholstered chairs.

The advantages are comfort, appearance, and improved acoustics. (Some acousticians contend that the padding in an upholstered chair will approximate the sound absorption of an occupied seat.) There are also those who contend that better seating warrants higher ticket prices.

Use of synthetic products has done much to extend the life of the covering materials used for seats and backs. Upholstered chairs are nevertheless subject to accidental damage and vandalism.

The formed plastic or "barrel-stave" seat is more economical and certainly more resistant to damage and normal wear. For outdoor facilities this seating is perhaps the only choice.

Whatever type seat is selected, care should be taken to ensure that support braces and other underparts permit unobstructed sweeping. Floor-mounted chairs would make arena maintenance almost economically impossible.

Some manufacturers feature cast-iron supports for their chairs; others used formed or pressed steel. The merits of both have been long debated. Both products, however, have records of long life and good performance. Figure 72 shows two types of fixed seating chairs.

Bleacher Seating

Although theaters and arenas customarily offer individual seats, outdoor facilities—and, indeed, some of the larger domed stadiums—achieve much of their capacity by the use of "bleacher" seating. Some of this seating provides backrests; others do not.

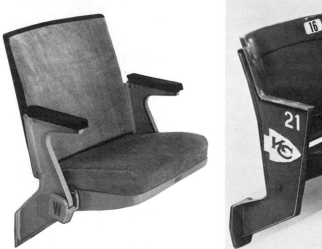

Figure 72. Although both chairs were designed as riser-mount types, the one on the left illustrates the fully upholstered models more commonly found in theaters and arenas. The one on the right is the molded type needed for outdoor stadiums. (American Seating Company.)

A bleacher is described as "an outdoor uncovered seat or stand for spectators." The most common form is perhaps a wide, sometimes plastic-coated board mounted on a seat form. Numbered spaces are usually marked off by painting stripes approximately 18 inches apart.

Comfort is not a by-product of bleacher seating. It is, however, economical, durable, and easily replaced. The use of bleachers produces the greatest capacity in the smallest space. Not only can "seats" be given the minimum width but no provision need be made for space between them. Normal practice places rows of bleacher seats substantially closer than rows of individual chairs, and a different rake or sightline may also be possible. Telescoping bleachers occupy the smallest amount of storage space when not in use.

At least one manufacturer is now offering conversion units by which individual plastic-formed chairs can be attached to the bleacher boards to provide improved seating. As stated by the American Seating Company engineers, chair-seat widths must be considered in any discussion of patron comfort and facility capacity. Although 18-inch widths were acceptable at one time, the industry has recognized the growth of its patrons and is now recommending widths in the range of 21 to 23 inches. Most arenas and theaters provide a variation in chair widths which serves as a means of staggering rows and fitting the chairs into the available space.

Basically, most fixed seating has two-piece construction. Adjustment of the backs is made at the time of manufacture or during installation. Seat cushions may be constructed of "foam" (i.e., polyethelene or polyurethane) padding or perhaps with springs. There may also be a combination of these components. The "polys" have virtually replaced all other padding, but such factors as density and thickness must be considered. Once all the air is expelled from the foam rubber, most of its resiliency will have gone. Testing the comfort of any chair should be undertaken only when there is time to remain seated on the cushion for a reasonable period of time.

Better seat cushions are, of course, constructed with springs. Some manufacturers recommend coil springs; others, serpentine. Both have their advantages and disadvantages.

Before leaving fixed seating, it must be pointed out that another style is the church pew. Customarily of wood construction, the pew combines support, seat, and back in one unit permanently fixed to the floor. Cushions, if any, are normally separate items. Here again economy, capacity, and undoubtedly tradition are the primary considerations.

Portable Chairs

The subject of portable or movable chairs is vastly more complex. The choice is greater and the possibility of accurately evaluating one against the other, difficult.

Disregarding "furniture-type" seating, office chairs, decorative benches, lobby furniture, and similar items for the moment, products of the major manufacturers can perhaps be roughly categorized into four basic types: sled, shell, tube frame, and folding.

What are the considerations?

Purpose.   What will be the chairs' major use or purpose? Will they augment the fixed seating in an arena? Will they be used for conventions and meetings or food functions? Are they the *only* movable chairs to be acquired? Must they be multipurpose?

Quantity.   If a larger number is needed, it may point toward the selection of a lower priced chair to meet budget limitations.

Appearance.   Perhaps not the most important factor, but one with great influence on buyer and user, is appearance. Style and design are varied and in some cases strongly affect function and other considerations.

Safety.   Safety for patrons, employees, and the facility itself is important. Liability claims are costly and can harm an establishment's reputation. Chairs should be checked for moving parts that may pinch fingers or tear clothing, for tipping when the occupant leans forward or back, and for stability when stacked.

Comfort.   For those who must spend several hours seated in one place comfort moves high on the list of considerations. A word of caution. When testing chairs for comfort, remain in the chair long enough for the cushion or pad to "bottom-out." When all the air is out of the cushion the comfort factor can be judged more accurately. The width and depth of the chair is as important as its height, particularly if it is to be used for dining.

Durability.   By their very nature portable chairs are moved frequently. They are folded, stacked, dropped, and often thrown. Patrons will rock on the back legs, sit on the backs, and stand on the seats. How the chairs are built to withstand these forms of abuse is important. Of almost equal concern is the ease or difficulty of repair. Selection of the proper upholstery material is essential.

Handling.   The man-power involved in handling portable chairs is a matter of great expense in most public facilities. Chairs must be taken from storage, set up, removed, placed in racks, and returned to storage. This factor should always be considered in chair selection. When joining or coupling is required, to meet fire and safety codes, operation of the ganging devices will have a telling effect on set-up and break-down time.

Storage.   The volume of storage space available for portable chairs must be considered. When several thousand chairs must be accommodated, the cubic footage of storage space takes on an impressive total. Folding chairs will normally require less storage space, although some unpadded stacking chairs can perhaps equal or exceed this capability.

It is also necessary to determine whether the chairs can be fitted in racks that can be stacked vertically, whether the racks can be handled by fork-lift trucks, whether the chairs will ride well and without damage when the racks are taken to storage, and what types of racks and moving equipment are available.

Price.   Initial investment is less important when all the other factors are considered. Budget limitations, however, are a fact of life and may well dictate the ultimate decision.

Chair Types

The following is a generalized description of portable chairs common to the present market:

Sled-type.   The sled-type chair has a tube, pipe, or heavy wire frame which is unique (see Figure 73) in that the tubes are formed in a continuous bar from front to back on each side to produce a sledlike base. These chairs have many good and bad points but one strong recommendation is their excellent stacking capability, especially those that have bodies of steel or plastic construction.

Shell.   The shell chair has tube, pipe, or wire legs and features a molded plastic body. The material may be known by a number of trade names but is basically some type of polyethelene, polyurethane, or polypropylene. Some come with fabric covers. A key concern is the quality and durability of the method by which the metal legs are connected to the plastic body (see figure 74).

Tube Frame.   As the name implies, a tube-frame chair is basically that. Formed tubing creates two leg frames; two more formed pieces—or sometimes one—make up the back frame. These three or four parts are then welded together. The seat and back are attached to the frame and the chair is complete. Seat and back pieces may be molded plastic but are usually padded (see Figure 75).

Figure 73. One of the four basic types of portable chair is the sled base. This base is favored by many for use on carpeted floors, for there are no glides or other protrusions to catch in the fiber. The sled base chair also permits a design that eliminates spans or cross bracing. (Fixtures Manufacturing Corp.)

Figure 74. In addition to its tubular steel frame, this chair has a one-piece "shell," seat/back made of high impact, flexible polypropylene. It is extremely light in weight and stacks well. (Fixtures Manufacturing Company.)

120

Figure 75. An excellent example of a highly popular stacking chair is this model manufactured by the Fixtures Manufacturing Company which comes in a wide range of styles, finishes, and fabrics. This particular model offers a leg-over-leg ganging system.

Figure 76. Two highly competitive folding chairs are the Krueger (shown on the left) and the Clarin. Both are offered in a variety of models with or without padded seats, with or without arms, independent lift seats, and other features.

Figure 77. Portable folding chairs present the best solution when storage is at a premium in public assembly facilities. This particular chair rack by Krueger can be rolled to a storage room and then hoisted by forklift to stack two or three high. The individual chairs, however, are handled only once. (Krueger)

Folding.   Folding chairs are offered in tube or pressed-steel construction. Seats and backs may be metal, sometimes wood, or completely upholstered (see Figure 76). They can be purchased with permanent or removable arms and are available with single arms for use in ganged rows. They can also be ordered with tablet arms for school use. Folding chairs have long been arena standbys because of their storage capabilities, ease of handling, and ability to withstand abuse (see Figures 77 and 78). Most manufacturers also make folding chairs with independent lift seats, a highly important feature when space is at a premium.

The following are a few other random points regarding chair selection:

In all arena, theater, or concert setups in which seats are reserved, it is necessary to identify the section, row, and seat. Because portable chairs rarely wind up in the same position twice, they must be numbered after each setup.

Folding chairs with lift seats usually provide a space on the underside in which a number can be chalked. Numbers printed on rolls of pressure-sensitive tape are commonly used on almost all other chairs. Good mainte-

Figure 78. Still another approach to compact storage of portable folding chairs is this floor truck which accommodates 72 chairs with padded seat cushions. (Clarin Corp.)

nance practice calls for the removal of the numbers after each event, for delay makes the job more difficult.

If the chairs are to be used for food functions, it would be wise to consider "waterfall" or "French" seams for the seat cushions in preference to welted seams which may catch particles of food.

Arms are available on many chair models. Although desirable for some events, chair arms may be somewhat restrictive to guests at large-scale food functions.

12. Admissions Control

Inherent to nearly all admission-type events is the need for efficient control of patrons. This control is also the concern of trade shows, conventions, and meetings of all kinds. Architectural planning and adequate equipment play an important role not only in the direction of the public but also in facility security.

Objectives are varied but public safety should be in the forefront. In addition, good admissions control and security programs must consider the interests of the promoter and ticket purchaser, crowd control, the security of exhibits, and the protection of the facility itself.

Public safety begins with good architectural planning, most of which is well covered by building and fire codes under government jurisdiction. To some extent management's need to guard the entrances and exits to restricted or ticketed areas may be in conflict with rapid evacuation in emergency circumstances. Regulations that may be necessary and acceptable *during* events may be costly nuisances in *nonevent* times, and intelligent compromises are often necessary to bring about workable solutions.

Of particular concern are the multipurpose complexes in which the interests of efficient management and public safety must be served. Important labor savings can be achieved by the use of folding gates, corridor barriers and other devices to assist in restricting the public from certain areas. By the same token, the use of such equipment can be authorized only under certain specific conditions.

Careful planning by the architect in cooperation with management consultants and fire prevention and/or insurance representatives should result in the development of the necessary flexibility of entrance patterns and emergency exit paths for a wide variety of events.

ADMISSIONS CONTROL

Admissions control in its simplest form is symbolized by the patron as he surrenders his ticket to a gateman and then moves along into the controlled area to enjoy the event.

Generally speaking, most admission-type events fall into two basic categories: *general admission,* which permits the patron to sit in any available seat, and *reserved,* for which the patron purchases a specific location.

For many events, particularly those offering general admission, patrons will often arrive early to be first in line. Depending on the circumstances, these early comers could be on hand anywhere from a few hours to a day ahead.

Needless to say, a sports arena or theater should have at least some covered, and preferably enclosed, areas outisde the main doors or turnstiles in which patrons may wait for the doors to open. Admission to the seating area generally begins approximately one hour before the advertised starting time.

Architectural planning must accept the fact that lines will form at ticket windows, turnstiles, and doors. It is impossible to predict their length, but intermingling of queues can lead only to confusion and possible trouble.

Once the patron has surrendered his ticket, he is handed a stub. If it is a general admission-type event, the stub represents a receipt that indicates payment of the entry fee. If the seats are reserved, stubs must carry section, row, and seat numbers.

Most large facilities employ lobby directors to help patrons find their way to the proper gates. Inside the turnstiles of many arenas and stadiums additional directors, or "splitters", offer further assistance to patrons.

In smaller facilities, such as theaters and concert halls, ushers may lead patrons directly to their seats. In larger arenas and stadiums, however, they are assigned to stations in major aisles to give patrons direction. Only when there is a problem does the usher leave his station.

Overseeing the activities of the staff of ushers will be one or more supervisors or head ushers whose responsiblity is to assist with extra heavy loads, settle ticket problems, or handle other matters that may need solving.

After intermission it is the responsibility of the ushers to see that patrons once again find their seats; at all times during the event they must answer questions, offer directions to rest rooms, concessions, and telephones, enforce smoking regulations, if any, watch for safety hazards, and assist any sick or injured persons to secure first aid or medical assistance.

In the event of an injury it is most important that the usher provide immediate assistance and summon professional help without delay. He can also be of great help by observing any conditions that may have contributed to the accident. An effort to obtain names and addresses of witnesses is also recommended. The volume of liability insurance claims has grown so rapidly in recent years that management has found it increasingly necessary to be informed of both valid and invalid situations.

Supporting the work of the ushers are security personnel who may be door guards, professional security guards, uniformed police, and/or staff watchmen. For rock music concerts the security staff may also include a cadre of strong-bodied young men equipped with an understanding of the crowd and wearing tee-shirts that identify them with the event or facility.

Security can be given immeasurable assistance by zoning the physical plant into areas of activity; for example, most facilities are divided into sections for the public, the performers, and service and support personnel.

Public areas are those spaces in which the public may move freely . . . after their tickets have been surrendered. The public area is also outside "control" or before the patron has presented his ticket, displayed a registration badge, or provided other identification. It should also contain a minimum of service functions.

Public areas inside admissions control must provide access to all facilities, concession areas, first aid stations, rest rooms, drinking fountains, and telephones. It should include all necessary accommodations without requiring access to other areas of the facility. Every effort should be made to discourage the need or desire to exit and return through controlled points.

Because smoking is not permitted in most theaters and in many arenas, public areas must be adequate within control perimeters to accommodate large crowds during intermissions.

Performer areas include "backstage," dressing rooms, costume storage rooms, and property rooms. These facilities must be as well separated from audience and service areas as is physically possible.

The need for privacy and sometimes protection for artists, athletes, and game officials is obvious. Whenever possible these areas should be separate even from those used by facility employees and other support personnel.

Costumes and show properties are uniquely valuable and irreplaceable within a reasonable time, once the show is on the road. For this reason many show contracts stipulate 24-hour surveillance.

Security personnel who are responsible for policing the backstage area must be carefully selected and trained. The physical setup should be such that under normal circumstances one person can screen all persons seeking admission and block any undesirables.

Service space includes carpenter and paint shops, custodial supply rooms, concessions commissary, receiving and shipping docks, engine room, locker rooms, and other areas directly involving personnel. All should be effectively secured from public access.

Support personnel areas are set aside for the use of door guards, gatemen, ushers, police, security officers, nurses and employees of a similar nature. These spaces, such as the first aid room, should be adjacent to public assembly areas but have access to "back-of-the-house" entry to permit personnel to enter and leave without disturbing the performance. Facility plans should also permit unobtrusive removal of persons requiring medical assistance or police detention.

An ideal arrangement is one that provides a single "back-of-the-house" entrance for building service personnel, athletes, and performers but with immediate separation of these individuals once inside the building. The location of time clocks, bulletin boards, receiving docks, and security personnel at a single employee entrance or stage door through which all personnel would enter and leave also reduces the possibility of loss of materials, supplies, and equipment.

CROWD CONTROL

Every event in a theater, arena, or stadium has its own personality. Each may attract an audience completely diverse from any other. Experienced facility administrators have learned that actions and reactions that soothe one audience can easily lead to riot conditions in another.

Many factors are involved. The type of performance or athletic event the performers or teams; whether there is general admission or all seats are reserved; the age of the audience; the presence of many small children; the time of day or night; length of performance; and on and on.

Obviously a symphony concert performed by mature established artists can be expected to bring out a well-dressed, disciplined audience interested primarily in seeing and hearing the performance. Ice shows and family shows are much the same, with the exception that the handling of small children may be a problem.

Athletic contests between two bitter rivals or a game in which much depends on the outcome can, however, result in substantially different audience reactions. Even so, normal security precautions and the use of readily available equipment will probably prove adequate for all but the most unusual problems.

Contemporary music or "hard rock" concerts usually require special crowd-control procedures to deal with this particular type of audience.

Because most rock concerts are performed in arenas or stadiums, large portable stages are required. Normal practice calls for a stage ranging in height from a minimum of 4 feet to perhaps 8 feet or more. The platform is customarily provided with a protective wood skirting to prevent overly enthusiastic admirers from attempting to reach the performers from below the stage. It has also been found advisable in specific cases to construct a barrier several feet in front of the stage, thus creating a dry moat or "no man's land" from which spectators are barred or immediately removed by security personnel.

Because these shows are frequently early sell-outs, the facility must be equipped with signs and a public address system with which to inform the public *outside* the building that no tickets are available. It becomes highly important to the security of the building and the safety of those who have bought tickets that adequate protection be provided against gate crashers.

TRADE SHOW SECURITY

Trade shows, convention exhibits, consumer shows, and product displays present equally challenging security problems. A first consideration, perhaps, is the nature of the event. Virtually all feature temporary displays or demonstrations of products and/or services and almost all employ the services of a show decorator and show electrician to provide such items as drapes, carpeting, furniture, and special utilities.

Generally speaking, trade shows serve a specific market; for example, a gift show that is open only to retail merchants or those "in the trade." Convention exhibits consist of products or services directed toward a particular profession or industry, and are usually restricted to registered delegates of the convention or specially invited guests. Neither is open to the general public.

Consumer shows are a different story. Home Shows, Boat Shows, Auto Shows, Recreation Vehicle Shows, and Sport Shows are designed for retailers to display their wares before the general public and perhaps even engage in direct selling in the hall. Admission is usually charged.

Product displays may be simple one-item exhibits in a heavily traveled area of a building or they may make up an entire exhibit hall of equipment in which dealers and retail merchants assemble to examine new products. The introduction of new cars in various regional centers are perhaps a good example of product display. Almost all are by invitation.

Admissions control is an important and necessary feature of most shows. If admission is charged, the patron will normally buy his ticket as he approaches the entrance to the exhibition. He then surrenders his ticket to a gateman and passes through a turnstile. He is usually permitted to move about freely among the displayed items, but is denied reentry if he leaves the hall.

Badges or special identification tickets form an important part of security control at all exhibits because of the large number of support personnel involved. In addition to building personnel, an exhibition may require the presence of representatives of the decorating contractor, not to mention the show electrician, maintenance employees, and the exhibitors themselves.

The general public at admission-type events or registered delegates at conventions are customarily admitted through the main gates. Exhibitors and employees are usually required to use a special entrance where their credentials and whatever items they may be carrying can be checked.

Theft, pilferage, and vandalism are primary problems in most trade shows. Losses are often more frequent among inexperienced or "trusting" exhibitors.

Trade show management generally informs all exhibitors that security for their displays is their own responsibility until the show opens officially. The responsibility is also the exhibitor's during the hours that the show is open to the public.

Most well-run shows require all exhibitors to obtain special permits to remove items from their displays during the show. All doors are guarded continuously, and patrons are required to leave by special exits. Patrons leaving the building by other means should be placed under surveillance. During nonshow hours doors are locked, alarmed, chained, or under visual observation.

When possible, exhibit hall exits should be grouped for a minimum of policing by security personnel. Exits that are hidden from direct view create difficult security problems and often require posting of special guards.

13. Box Office Procedures

Box office operations are a vital function of all audience support activities. It is here that many patrons have their closest contact with facility personnel, and it is here that architectural provisions must be made to provide good service and at the same time allow uninterrupted pedestrian flow through the main entrance.

Perhaps because of a lack of understanding or failure to grant ticket offices a sufficiently high priority, these spaces have all too often become the "stepchildren" of the facility. Early correction or alteration is often required after the building has opened.

Some of the major planning errors include an insufficient number of ticket windows, lack of weather protection for ticket purchasers, inadequate working space, insufficient security and privacy, improper location, and shortages of electrical outlets and telephone connections.

The importance of proper box office space has been pushed forward in recent years as management of more and more facilities has opted or been forced to undertake ticket selling. Although it was once almost entirely an independent enterprise, surveys indicate that more than 60 % of all facilities responding now provide on-site ticket-handling service. It appears reasonable to assume that this trend will continue.

Basic needs are much the same no matter who operates the box office. Space is required for the advance sale of tickets, day-of-event sales, ticket storage, and accounting. A room is also needed for handling mail orders and accepting telephone orders or answering inquiries.

The main box office layout should contain several advance sale windows, depending to a great degree on the size and nature of the facility. In most cases these windows open onto the main lobby. Additional spaces include a counting room, vault or safe, telephone room, mail-order room, storage space, manager's office, and one other room in which representatives of the show may examine and verify the manager's reports.

Whenever possible, one ticket window should open toward the interior of the building to permit inquiries or possible exchange of seats without requiring the patron to pass through a turnstile or some other control point.

The most functional operations are those that make it possible to move all ticket sales to individual ticket booths or kiosks immediately before a performance. Patrons arriving to buy tickets for the current performance may be separated from those asking for advanced sales.

Individual box offices normally accommodate one or two sellers. Their requirements are reasonably simple. Windows should be located to permit standing lines to form and should be large enough to give the seller a view of those waiting. A small shelf on which to handle tickets, a cash drawer, good lighting, and a telephone or intercom are all the equipment that is needed. Heat and/or air conditioning may be required, depending on the location. A single doorway with a strong lock is adequate. At least one or more box offices must provide special accommodations for handicapped persons.

All selling stations must be equipped with speaker holes at the proper height in the window and an opening at counter height, designed to preclude anyone from reaching through, for passing tickets and money. Slatted metal closures for the windows are a safety measure when box offices are closed, and bullet proof glass is commonplace in some areas.

In advance ticket sale offices sellers require ample front counter space with cash drawers and storage space below. Ticket racks are often placed on the counter to speed selling at certain events. The major supply of reserved seat tickets, however, is stored in ticket racks mounted on the back wall directly behind the sellers. (This requirement, of course, is substantially modified when a computerized ticketing system is installed.)

The counting room will require electric plug strips or some method of providing outlets in a number of locations. Counter space or work tables are needed for several persons.

The security of all box offices cannot be overemphasized. Not only must unsold tickets be protected at all times but substantial sums of cash will be on hand during many hours of the day and night. Box office personnel other than ticket sellers must be beyond public view and provision must be made so that visitors can be screened before box office doors are opened. A security alarm system is essential.

The ticket office facilities described here apply primarily to arena operations. Much the same is required for auditoriums and theaters but on a smaller scale.

COMPUTERIZED TICKETING SYSTEMS

Computerized ticketing for sports events and entertainment have made, and can be expected to make, enormous changes in box office operations and procedures. Planners of new facilities should investigate the possibility that management will go this route.

Computerized ticket equipment is currently available, and it seems more than probable that the industry will gradually move in this direction.

Initially the concept called for a central computer in one location with terminals in other cities controlled from that point. The newer systems, however, provide for a central unit in each city and remote sales locations throughout the area. Also available are "minisystems" that provide on-site computerized ticketing with no remote outlets.

Computer ticket systems consist basically of one or more central processor units, console controls equipped with video screens, high speed line printers, and ticket printing machines. Thus an operator can determine what events are on sale, ask for the best seats available at a given price, location, or performance, and then print the tickets for immediate sale and delivery to the patron. The same capability is available at the box office or at a remote location many miles away.

Accounting and recordkeeping is automatic. A daily settlement or report on the status of any or all events can be delivered on command.

The computer eliminates press printing of tickets which has been common practice for many years. It also eliminates counting-in and storing tickets as well as counting "deadwood" or unsold tickets after the close of the event. Not only is security vastly improved but substantial reductions in labor costs are realized.

Several arenas in the United States now own and operate their own computer ticket systems, and the availability of the smaller, one-unit system has brought the cost within range of even small performing arts centers.

Shifting of box office operations to computerized ticketing will probably mean less storage and counting room area but more space and electric power near the selling windows. In fact, ticket windows of the future may resemble today's airline ticket counter.

14. Concessions

By most definitions the term "concession" is considered a subsidiary business conducted by lease or purchase of privilege. Some state that a concession is "the lease of premises for a particular purpose."

There are within the typical public assembly facility many concessions—parking, box office, trade show services, and so on. For purposes of this chapter, however, focus is made on the most common use of the term, which is for fast foods and beverages.

Food and beverage service at seated functions, such as luncheons and banquets, is discussed in a subsequent chapter under the heading of "Catering."

The importance of good concessions operation to the average arena or stadium cannot be overemphasized. The role of the concessions department drops proportionately with the size of the facility to the point that it may be of only slight concern in many performing arts centers.

Rarely is an arena, auditorium, or stadium financially successful without the efficient operation of concessions. If the public decides that its entertainment and recreational needs are being properly served, it will return time and time again. The *total* experience, however, must be consistently satisfactory.

Percentages vary, but all arenas and stadiums report concessions revenues as an important and vital part of total volume.

A key question facing policy makers of both public and private facilities is whether concessions should be operated by the building or leased to a contractor. If leased, on what basis should the contractor be selected and for what period of time? Should concessions equipment be bought by the building or the concessions contractor? Finally, what controls should management exercise over the contractor?

A move has been noted in the auditorium/arena field during the last decade toward self-operation of concessions by facilities. The shift has been slow, and surveys continue to show that in the majority of buildings the concessions rights are leased to individuals or operating companies.

It should also be noted that the percentage of facilities with leased concessions appears to gain in direct proportion to the size of the facility.

Many managers who favor leasing point out that a firm whose business is operating concessions has better and more experienced personnel, full time to devote to this activity, the advantage of mass purchasing power, better operating controls, and the financial resources to make necessary expenditures and capital investments.

On the other side of the ledger, those favoring self-operation contend that their system brings not only better control but also a higher percentage of profit. Although self-operation may add 10 to 15% more net revenue than could be expected from a lessee, it does at the same time require a substantial capital investment in equipment.

Professional concessions operators explain that although self-operation may result in a higher percentage of net profit a smaller percentage of a higher gross figure may in the final analysis give the facility more dollars. It is the position of the professional operator that his expertise and marketing capabilities will produce higher sales revenues.

Surveys by the International Association of Auditorium Managers indicate that amounts paid by concessionaires to buildings range between 15 and 40%; 25 to 30% appears to be the current average paid in facilities in which beer and/or liquor is *not* permitted and 32 to 35% is about average where their sale *is* approved.

All things being equal, a building can undoubtedly operate its concessions at a higher profit margin than private enterprise. If nothing else, a publicly owned facility usually need not concern itself with tax matters. The key determination is whether building management can operate the concessions department as efficiently or perhaps better than a private operator. This decision will require careful evaluation of the manager's capabilities and those of his staff in the concessions field.

These evaluations relate more particularly to large facilities. Generally it would appear that smaller buildings and theaters would perhaps be better served by self-operation. Two factors that influence this decision may be the absence of qualified local concessionaires and lack of interest on the part of national operators because of limited revenue potentials.

Although somewhat contrary to a profit-oriented approach, some buildings operate their concessions in order to control and perhaps deemphasize them; for example, some theaters and concert halls limit their sales to cold drinks and then only under restricted conditions, selling before the performance and at intermission. Patrons are not permitted to take drinks to their seats and sales are made only in lobbies and concourses at stands or vending machines. Under these restrictions, which result in low per capita sales, it is doubtful that any commercial concessionaire would be interested in operating such a facility.

No matter who operates the concessions, the requirements for success remain much the same. The stands must be attractive, clean, and sanitary and employees must be courteous and neatly uniformed; properly prepared, quality products must be served with variety and at fair prices and service must be rapid and efficient.

Although merchandising techniques will vary, arenas and stadiums utilize fairly standardized types of facility. The most common, of course, is the fixed or portable snack stand.

A study by *Amusement Business* made several years ago showed that 90% of the stadiums and 88% of the arenas and auditoriums operated refreshment stands. It is reasonable to assume that the figures will change little, other than to move more strongly in this direction.

Vending machines are becoming more common in all facilities but their usefulness is more for supplementing normal stand activities. Their greatest benefit is felt at minor events, and at nonpeak periods.

Most major stadiums and sports arenas also employ vendors. These are "hawkers" or "butchers" who offer products for sale in the seated areas. In larger facilities they produce good results and are highly important in creating large per capita receipts. These sellers usually work on a commission based on gross sales.

Under normal circumstances vendors are needed to maximize sales. This is particularly true when patrons are reluctant to leave their seats at events with continuity of action, such as football, hockey, and soccer. Well-designed facilities with wide aisles and short rows plus convenient access to

A 1969 survey by *Amusement Business* classifies food and drink facilities throughout North America.

	Auditoriums and Arenas	Stadiums
Refreshment stands	88%	90%
Vending machines	62	23
Mobile concession stands	40	42
Restaurants (sit-down)	14	17
Cafeterias (with tables)	13	20
Kitchen facilities	41	22
Outside catering	40	30
Vendors	22	34

Source: *Amusement Business.*

concession stands could perhaps be operated without vendors, but because these conditions are not generally found the vendor has become a necessity. It is incumbent on management, therefore, to insist on courteous and efficient service with a minimum of interference to the spectators.

In exhibition halls the concessionaire will often set up tables and chairs in conjunction with portable or permanent snack bars. This arrangement is usually well received by show management, exhibitors, and patrons alike, many of whom have spent many hours walking around the hall. Because the concessionaire is not faced with impact crowds that exist during half-time intermissions, he can often add a few special items to the menu.

CONCESSION STANDS

The importance of concession stands to the financial welfare of the building and the enjoyment of the patrons cannot be overstated. Their location and size are also matters of concern. Far too often in planning public assembly facilities, concessions stands have been shoved behind or under some other feature of the building and the concessionaires have been left to do the best they could with the space available.

Proper merchandizing requires colorful and neatly organized stands. The counters, back bars, graphics, and uniforms must be color-coordinated, and space and equipment for mass display of merchandise must be provided to promote impulse buying. Adequate storage and preparation space is also needed. This is critically important during peak periods in order that serving areas may be quickly restocked when supplies run low (see Figures 79 and 80).

A leading national concessionaire points out that to be effective stands should be conveniently located to all seats. A patron should be able to reach the nearest stand in 40 to 60 seconds. The size of the stand is not nearly so significant as the convenience to the customer. General recommendations state that some 36 linear feet of front counter and about 650 square feet overall is ideal for the average stand. Approximately 6 square feet of auxiliary space for each linear foot of front counter is also desirable.

Another generalization used in determining the size of refreshment stands is the suggestion that 20 to 25 linear feet of counter be allotted for every 1000 seats if vending is not permitted. With vending, about 7 feet less per 1000 persons would be acceptable (see Figure 81).

Figure 79. Larger concession stands are normally required for such facilities as Arrowhead Stadium in Kansas City at which heavy "impact" crowds must be served during half-time intermissions. In this setup the patrons are required to queue under the pointed fingers for service. All products on the menu are available at each station. Note that only drinks and popcorn are on the front counter. All other items are on the back counter or located immediately below the service counter. (Courtesy of Volume Service.)

Figure 80. Extremely well designed, finished, and equipped, this concession stand service box seat ticket holders located behind home plate at Cincinnati's Riverfront Stadium. The brick front, plus generous use of wood and decorative lighting, gives the stand a unique appearance. (Courtesy of Sportservice Corporation.)

Placement of equipment such as high-speed beverage units, food warmers, and other items is as important as the selection of equipment itself. The operation should be organized so that all items can be quickly served by a single person at each selling station. This not only eliminates confusion and interference among stand workers but ensures speedier, one-stop service to patrons (see Figure 82).

For security, sanitary, and other reasons it is important that snack stands be equipped with positive locking capabilities. All stands require full utilities with the possible exception of natural gas. Venting of each stand will provide greater flexibility in determining the menus to be offered. It is also important that special heating and/or cooling equipment be provided when circumstances dictate. A substantial volume of heat generated by numerous appliances may be trapped inside by the configuraiton of the space. In some locations during cold weather it may be difficult to maintain even temperatures in stands facing exterior doors.

Figure 81.   Facing the same problem as concessions stands, bars in arenas and stadiums must be prepared to handle "impact" crowds during intermissions and other breaks in play. This large installation employs decorative lighting and color as opposed to graphics to attract patrons at Cincinnati's Riverfront Stadium. (Courtesy of Sportservice Corporation.)

SELECTING A CONCESSIONAIRE

Concessions contracts for publicly owned facilities are awarded on the basis of competitive bidding. As a general rule the operator who offers the highest bid and otherwise meets all requirements is given the rights.

In privately owned buildings in particular contracts are negotiated after interviews have been held with a number of potential contractors. Both methods have produced highly successful operations.

As a guideline, most facilities have drafted specifications that describe the general conditions of the operation, the responsibilities of the concessionaire, the authority of management, standards expected, bonding and insurance requirements, reporting and audit provisions, and other legal requirements. These specifications become a part of the contract document.

In addition to the customary bid factors of percentages to be paid and

Figure 82. Attention-grabbing graphics attract patrons to concession stands in both arenas and stadiums. Most stand layouts provide single-station arrangements similar to this one in which the patron comes to a designated point and the stand attendant provides all items on the menu without excess movement. This particular stand offers draft beer. (Courtesy of Volume Service.)

other items, owners of many new facilities have found it advantageous to require bidders to specify the amount of money they will spend to provide proper equipment.

The term of the concessions contract will depend on the amount of the initial equipment investment, policies of the governing authority and prevailing government regulations. Surveys indicate that about 25% are two-to-three-year contracts and the balance for longer periods. The larger facilities and major concessions companies appear to favor the longer terms.

A primary reason for the longer contracts in larger facilities, of course, is to provide the concessionaire with a reasonable opportunity to amortize the equipment he is required to install. In some cases this sum can run anywhere from $500,000 to $2,000,000 or more.

In developing a contract, it is well to provide the administrative authority with some mechanism by which the term of the agreement can be extended when a qualified operator has demonstrated his competence and willingness to perform the services required. Many government jurisdictions have regulations that require periodic rebidding following which contracts are awarded to the highest bidder. In concessions operation, however, this process can work to the detriment of the owner and lead to the better operators being gradually pushed out of contention.

If the local system, even though it has been instituted for fine and logical reasons, calls for periodic rebidding and if management or the governing authority is not permitted to act on the proposal that is in the best interests of the facility and the public, it follows that a competitor will quickly realize that he has only to offer a higher, even if unrealistic, percentage in order to acquire the concessions rights. Conversely, if the current operator is paying a fair percentage and producing good grosses, it may be all that the facility administrators can reasonably expect.

Awarding the bid to an operator who has offered more than he can practically afford may mean he can survive only by cutting corners, decreasing quality, reducing service, or possibly making other even more drastic moves.

As a criterion, it would appear that once a facility has developed a successful concessions operation and is assured of receiving an equitable percentage of receipts, every effort should be made to stabilize the operation rather than to press for extra percentage points.

PER CAPITA EXPENDITURES

It may be useful to mention briefly the subject of per capita expenditures in regard to concessions. As stated earlier, sports events far outdistance all other activities.

Many factors have a bearing on per capita spending and most facilities and/or concessionaires keep close tabs on these data.

Some of the variables are the following:

- Type of event
- Facility Design
- Appearance of the concessions operation
- Weather
- Crowd enthusiasm
- Performance of the home team
- Merchandising methods
- Time of day
- Hours of the event
- Menu prices

- Efficiency of concessions employees
- Number of intermissions

Some generalizations: per capita spending at sports events is highest; outdoor events usually achieve higher per capita figures; including of beer or liquor on the menu will move totals even higher.

Surveys indicate the per capita spending is best for baseball, followed by football, boxing, hockey, basketball, circuses, exhibitions, concerts, and ice shows.

15. Food and Beverages

Although fast foods from concession stands and vendors may meet the needs of most arenas and stadium patrons, they fall far short of the far-reaching requirements of modern-day conference and convention centers. Almost without exception the food and beverage demands of such facilities are comparable with those of first-class hotels and restaurants.

For our purposes—and with apologies for generalization—food and beverage functions are those at which guests are seated. It may be breakfast, luncheon, dinner, or banquet, but in any event table service of some sort is provided.

In most facilities this service is categorized as "catering," regardless of whether foods are prepared on-site or elsewhere.

In the average convention facility the primary needs for the service of food stem from two principal sources. One, the building may represent the only place in the city at which the required number of delegates can be served simultaneously; two, the meeting planner knows that attendance at convention sessions is greatly improved if registrants can be served at the site.

Perhaps a third reason is that the convention hall is a common meeting ground for delegates and on-site luncheons are therefore better attended. This may be particularly true when hotel accommodations are severely fragmented.

Establishment of the size and capacity of the banquet or assembly hall where major food functions will be held calls for close analysis of the potential market, an inventory of existing or competing facilities, and a check of the marketability of the hall for local uses. In many situations one or more major annual events may serve to point toward desirable or acceptable maximums.

KITCHENS

Perhaps one of the early administrative policy decisions faced by most owners may be whether to provide a full kitchen or merely a catering kitchen for food prepared elsewhere.

Many factors must be considered in determining the size and capability of any kitchen. The frequency of use and volume of food to be served must be estimated. The size of the community in which the facility is located and the existence of competing or supporting restaurants are of equal importance. The availability of a production kitchen within an acceptable distance must also be considered. Unfortunately, political or business influences may also affect the final decision.

It is interesting that most of the major convention facilities in North America and virtually all of those in Europe are equipped with full production kitchens and the necessary support spaces. It should also be noted that an undetermined but impressive number of facilities have been opened with catering kitchens, only to be converted later—and perhaps inadequately—to full production.

The dilemma has sometimes been resolved by providing adequate space for a full production kitchen and then equipping it for catering until the time that the needs of the potential market could be determined. In borderline areas or politically difficult situations this may be the most appropriate approach. Recent surveys show that more than 55% of all auditorium and arena facilities have at least installed catering kitchens. The percentage leaps when older buildings and campus facilities are extracted from the overall totals.

Quantitative space requirements for kitchen, servery, storage, dishwashing, and other support space will depend on many factors and should be properly determined by professional consultants specializing in this field.

Typical equipment to be found in a catering kitchen includes such basic items as a dishwasher, large steam table or bain-marie, coffee-makers, and reach-in coolers. These would, of course, be augmented by adequate electric outlets for portable food warmers plus work tables. The same equipment would undoubtedly be needed if later the kitchen is escalated to a full production operation. In addition, necessary storage space will be needed for china, glassware, silver, and linen.

The location of the kitchen in the complex is, of course, of great importance. Food-preparation and serving areas should be placed as close as possible to the major dining spaces but at the same time must have adequate access to receiving docks and trash disposal.

Employee entrances in the general area of food handling are desirable, as is space to accommodate the personal belongings of kitchen personnel. If possible, a separate entrance for catering personnel is recommended, for this department may be required to work on schedules substantially different from others in the building.

BANQUET TABLES

Banquet tables, chairs, head table risers, and stages are usually the property of the hall and are set up by building personnel for use by the caterer.

Convention hall equipment will usually include not only 6- and 8-foot banquet tables but also 60- or 72-inch round tables, for the latter have gained substantially in popularity in recent years. A rule-of-thumb in the industry suggests that a dining area will accommodate one person for each 10 to 11 square feet of floor space. This may prove accurate for rectangular tables but a multiplier of about 12 square feet per person is more realistic when round tables are employed or when a substantial amount of room is occupied by a large stage or head table arrangement.

Generally speaking, 6-foot rectangular tables will seat six persons each; 8-foot rectangulars will accomodate eight people. The 48-inch round tables are recommended fo seating four to six persons, 60-inch rounds for eight to 10 persons and 66-inch rounds for 10 to 12 persons.

Head-table platforms come in a wide variety of lengths and widths. The method of construction and combinations vary, but basically all provide a means of raising rectangular tables anywhere from 6 to 48 inches above the floor. Steps, table skirting, and safety guard rails are a part of the riser equipment and must be installed in accordance with local and/or building safety regulations.

Speakers' lecterns, also customarily the property of the facility, come in basically two heights: a table lectern which sits on the head table and a floor lectern which stands free. On some of the floor models heights may be adjusted mechanically.

FULL-TIME RESTAURANTS

Many of the newer convention centers are incorporating full-time restaurants, cafeterias and/or cocktail lounges as an integral part of program and design. When capital construction funds are available and the potential market exists, such facilities serve convention delegatres well. Even so, they must be developed to serve the public under impact conditions. The operator can often expect most of his customers to arrive almost simultaneously, for they have been attending the same meeting or function. By the same token, most will have to return to the next meeting or session at the same hour. In some buildings this problem has been met by adding a self-service cafeteria to a more conventional restaurant.

Construction and design of dining facilities appear to be much the same as in other well-equipped commercial restaurants, with the possible exception that most are designed to expand or contract, depending on the size of the meeting underway.

In many facilities in which construction of a permanent restaurant has not been possible because of space restrictions, lack of funds, or perhaps the absence of a dependable schedule of events, the intermittent food and beverage demands of convention and other groups are met with portable or temporary setups. Facility management generally provides the tables and chairs and perhaps even lays carpeting. Portable steam tables and other serving counters are then moved in to provide cafeteria or buffet service.

This highly desirable flexibility permits the exhibit or convention manager to establish a dining area wherever it best fits the needs of the exhibit. In most cases the portable setups can function adequately with existing utilities and the possible addition of heavy-duty power. A nearby source of water is a plus feature but not normally critical.

OPERATING PROCEDURES

In addition to consideration of a catering versus a full production kitchen will be the decision to make catering rights exclusive or nonexclusive.

Under an exclusive arrangement qualified caterers are invited to bid for the right to operate for a specified number of years. Candidates must state the percentage of gross receipts from food and beverage sales that they propose to pay the hall and may be asked to specify an amount to be invested in operating equipment. Experience and qualifications must also be substantiated.

Listed are some of the advantages accruing to the hall from an exclusive catering arrangement:

- A dependable food and beverage service for events of all sizes.
- A single organization on which may be fixed the responsibility for quality.
- A single organization to whom management can look for the care and maintenance of property and equipment.
- Supervision and possible control of prices.
- Marketing assistance.
- A source of capital investment in kitchen equipment.
- A single organization to be responsible for compliance with local liquor laws.

Opponents of the exclusive catering plan are quick to point out that such an arrangement deprives the lessee of a choice of caterer and also denies him the opportunity to seek competitive bidding on each food function.

A nonexclusive program, however, has often resulted in unwarranted criticism of the facility after an organization has been given poor food and service by a low-bid caterer. More often than not the guest at a food function is totally unaware of the caterer's identity. He only knows that he has had an unpleasant experience and blames it on the building.

Many facilities, and particularly those in the convention industry, have found it necessary to establish certain high standards of quality in order to attract and retain business. These goals are impossible if the lessee is permitted to use price as his only criterion in the selection of a food caterer.

It is sometimes difficult for management to impose and collect a percentage payment on nonexclusive caterers because of the lack of formal agreements and the further lack of accounting mechanisms. Sanitation and the care of equipment may be serious problems under a nonexclusive plan. All caterers who use building facilities are expected to leave them in mint condition. Such matters, however, often prove subjective and may lead to troublesome disputes. Short-time caterers may also have trouble arranging for the proper disposition of trash and garbage.

The nonexclusive concept proves almost unworkable under any circumstances in which a facility has more than one dining area. Customarily only one kitchen is provided and when two or more lessees select their own caterers for a particular date and time conflicts of all kinds can be expected.

It should also be noted that minor activities or meetings that perhaps require only coffee service are of little interest to caterers. Under nonexclusivity, management may be hard-pressed to provide it. Under an exclusive plan caterers must handle all requests, both large and small. In smaller communities the matter of catering exclusivity may become extremely sensitive when local residents demand the right to schedule "pot-luck" dinners or to serve food prepared by volunteer organizations.

Despite the worthiest intentions, volunteer or amateur operations are usually incompatible with the overall responsibilities and objectives of a facility. Experienced managers point out that someone still has to provide the coffeemakers and other kitchen equipment; someone must do the cleaning; someone must be responsible for accidents to those working in the kitchen; someone must be responsible for the purity of the food; and so on. Finally, if enough business cannot be generated to support the activities of a professional caterer, the building may then find itself incapable of providing quality food and beverage service on a stable basis.

In many situations facility owners or operators have found it highly desirable to write combined catering and concessions contracts and thus make only one firm responsible for all food and beverage service, regardless of type or size.

16. Operation and Maintenance

Although usually unnoticed among the cheers of the crowds and the glamor of the stars, facility operation, maintenance, and housekeeping are nevertheless the basic responsibilities of management. The presence of clean floors and well-maintained equipment may not always be mentioned by lessees and patrons but their absence will certainly be obvious.

Because of the increasing number of entertainment/convention complexes throughout North America, the necessity for high standards of maintenance and service has become ever more apparent. Promoters and convention planners have many choices of location. No longer must they accept dirty run-down facilities.

Throughout the industry three basic systems of maintenance appear to have evolved over the years. The first, and perhaps most common, is an *in-house* staff employed by the facility. Another is sometimes termed a *skeleton* staff on which only management representatives are permanent employees. The third system is represented by a *maintenance* contract. There are, of course, combinations of all three. The *in-house* staff is structured with sufficient full-time personnel to meet the needs of daily operation. Supplemental requirements are met by using them on an overtime basis or by bringing in part-time workers.

For busy facilities an in-house staff may prove the only answer to the heavy demands of daily setups and breakdowns, cleaning, and maintenance. In addition, management is guaranteed steady help as well as direct control. There is also the benefit to be gained from the experience of well-trained employees, particularly by those facilities that cater to conventions or other events that require special attention.

The *skeleton* staff is usually comprised of management and enough regular personnel to meet the day-to-day demands of the building, particularly during slow times and on non-event days. Standing by are part-time custodians, maintenance people, and event personnel who may come from any number of sources such as a city labor pool, employment offices, or contract services. For buildings in smaller communities with intermittent activities the skeleton staff has worked well by holding salary budgets to the minimum.

The *maintenance contract* may call for all supervision and labor to be provided by a contracting company. A key advantage cited by proponents of the system is the avoidance of direct union negotiations and conflicts.

These matters, as well as recruitment and provision of fringe benefits, are the responsibility of the contractor. In some political jurisdictions in which administrators of public facilities find it difficult to resist union demands, the contract system may be of great value.

A disadvantage of the contract method is the loss of direct control over personnel and possibly a less-than-satisfactory level of maintenance and service.

OPERATION AND MAINTENANCE OBJECTIVES

Management of audience support facilities must develop a delicate balance between operation and maintenance because their business is on-going and both maintenance and custodial work must be performed without interruption of the operation schedule.

Basically, each event in an arena or flat-floor facility requires a new setup. This may mean laying a basketball court, freezing an ice rink, setting up a portable stage or several thousand chairs. Conversion from basketball to hockey or from a concert hall to dining room must often be done in a matter of hours, and a lack of proper advance architectural planning can do much to add to operational costs.

Once the hall is set and ready for the use by a particular event management is faced with providing proper lighting, heating and/or cooling, restroom facilities, and other amenities for the comfort and safety of the public. At the close of the event there is the task of sweeping hundreds of rows and aisles and disposing of yards of trash—primarily waste from concessions products sold during the performance—hand mopping of aisles, machine scrubbing of corridors and major flat areas, cleaning of restrooms, employee support spaces, offices, lobbies and exterior portions of the facility.

The process is then begun all over again by setting up for the next event!

Summer months are normally the slowest of the year for most facilities, and it is then that management schedules major repairs or construction that would call for closing down all or part of the building. Regardless of the system chosen, much of its success or failure depends on the skill and experience of the facility's operations manager. The title may vary from "operations director" to "building superintendent" to "assistant manager" but the responsibilities are the same. Once an activity has been scheduled, this person is responsible for preparing the house, supervising operations during the event, and cleaning up after it is over.

Proper facility planning requires the location of storage space as near as possible to the areas in which the equipment will be used. The less time required for equipment in transit, the faster and cheaper the setup. Convenient location of janitor closets and supply stations can also serve to reduce labor costs.

Daily cleaning is a special concern. Architects should give attention to the selection and specification of materials for floors, walls, ceilings, and equipment that will result in a minimum of maintenance and repair. The same study should be given to plumbing fixtures, light fixtures, hardware, and other items; for example, to facilitate scrubbing restrooms should be equipped with ceiling-hung toilet partitions as opposed to floor-mounted dividers and doors; arena seats should be mounted high enough on risers to permit easy sweeping beneath the chairs.

Planners must be aware that a hefty pile of trash can accumulate under each row of seats. The seating plan must provide access for the collection and disposal of these waste materials.

Experienced managers have cautioned architects to avoid specification of specially designed lighting fixtures or other equipment that cannot be readily replaced or repaired. Complicated paint formulas that are difficult or expensive to duplicate should also be avoided.

HOUSEKEEPING

A high quality of custodial maintenance goes as far, perhaps, as any other single feature to establish a building's favorable public image. Still, it is all too often overlooked in administrative evaluations or in the establishment of management criteria.

Unfortunately custodial work by its very nature is not often conducive to the highest employee morale. Consequently, good equipment and materials and pleasant working conditions will go far toward improving the attitudes of these staff members. Operations and maintenance personnel should be reminded repeatedly of the importance of their work in the overall facility performance.

As so ably demonstrated by such pioneer amusement parks as Tivoli Gardens and Disneyland, good housekeeping and cleanliness are "contagious." Strategically placed refuse containers and the presence of active custodial workers during public events can do much to suggest to everyone that their help will be appreciated in keeping the facility clean and devoid of unnecessary litter.

Public assembly facilities, particularly those catering to sports activities and rock music concerts, are subject to heavy usage, frequent equipment damage, and vandalism. As a result it is the responsibility of the custodial crew to be aware of and report any items of equipment or structure that need repairing. This maintenance work should be performed as rapidly as possible, for proper care can do much to lengthen the life of expensive equipment.

Because most repairs will be handled by building personnel, the need is readily apparent for shops equipped to perform carpentry, welding, painting, and similar work. In many jurisdictions, however, safety and fire regulations require that they be separately housed.

The matter of security of equipment and supplies must be kept in mind at all times. Facilities of this nature are occupied not only by their own employees but by those of lessees as well and by the general public. It has been said that locks keep only the honest honest—but that at least is a place to start.

17. Dressing Rooms

Unseen by the public and often given insufficient consideration by planners, dressing rooms are nevertheless far more than basic necessities in any audience support facility.

To artists, performers, and athletes the dressing room becomes a base of operations. Depending on the nature of an individual's performance, the need may be great or merely a convenience. No matter whether an artist makes full use of it for makeup and costume changes, his performance, attitude, and regard for a given facility or community may well be affected by the quality, location, security, and cleanliness of the dressing room.

SPORTS-ORIENTED FACILITIES

Because of their variety of uses, arenas present one of the strongest challenges to facility planners in researching the number, type and size of dressing rooms required.

154

The most common need in arenas and stadiums is for *team* dressing rooms. In an arena a minimum of four rooms is generally acceptable for accommodating players during double-header games, tournaments, and similar events.

For facilities that serve as home base for professional, or perhaps even collegiate, teams consideration should be given to providing additional dressing rooms which can be assigned to them on a full-time, uninterrupted basis.

Determination of specific dressing room sizes will depend on many factors. Certain sports such as hockey and football require substantially more player equipment than others. As a result, facilities catering to these activities will require greater square footage of dressing room space per player than others.

The size of player rosters is still an additional factor. Home teams, for example, can usually be expected to "dress" more players than visiting squads.

Still another matter to be considered is the status or proficiency level of the teams that may be expected to use the dressing rooms. Team owners, coaches, and players have come to assume that dressing rooms in a particular league or conference will have similar standards. Dressing rooms of professional teams or those of major collegiate athletic conferences, however, offer more comforts and amenities than do those of some municipal facilities, small colleges, or high schools.

Planners would be well advised to be familiar with the dressing room "standards" of the conferences or leagues for which they are designing facilities.

All dressing rooms will require a changing area with stalls or hangers for clothing, showers, drying rooms, tables for taping, and toilets. Special floor coverings to protect skate blades or cleats and prevent slipping are another dressing room requirement.

Perhaps the best designed dressing rooms catering to any sport are those with independent heating and cooling systems. With such controls, a dressing room may be comfortably cooled when crowded with players and then later heated for rapid drying of equipment. Special attention must be paid to an exhaust system capable of quickly removing stale air and odors from dressing rooms.

Metal lockers with doors may be necessary in educational institutions and athletic clubs but their use should be discouraged in facilities catering to transient teams. In most public buildings such lockers are rarely used and in many cases have been removed.

Baseball, football, basketball, and hockey trainers almost unanimously recommend stalls equipped with a bench or stool, hangers, a shelf, and possibly a lockable box or vault for valuables. These stalls provide space for the player's clothing during the game or practice session and a place in which equipment can dry afterward.

Attention should also be given to slightly higher benches for basketball teams because of the generally greater height of these athletes.

Adjacent to team dressing rooms—and protected from the general public—should be a first aid room especially designed for athletes. Facilities catering to hockey and football will undoubtedly require more sophisticated first aid rooms and equipment than others because of the nature of injuries common to those sports.

Professional teams require at least some conditioning and therapeutic equipment. Whenever possible, clubs provide heat treatments, massage, and saunas.

An ideal arrangement for facilities housing two or more professional clubs is a design that incorporates separate dressing rooms, coaches offices, and storage areas for each team adjacent to a common space for training and physical conditioning.

A lounge in which players may gather before games and after practice or meet their families and friends after a game is a most satisfactory arrangement.

Augmenting team dressing rooms should be several smaller dressing rooms for groups of four to five persons plus a number of still smaller personal or "star" dressing rooms large enough for one or two artists. All rooms should contain shower stalls and toilets. Mirrors, good lighting and a dressing table or shelf are standard. Drawers can be equipped with hasps so that a performer can safeguard his valuables with his own padlock.

Determination of the specific number of dressing rooms to be provided will depend on the events for which the building is designed and on the proximity of additional space in hallways or adjacent meeting rooms that can be converted to dressing room use for events such as ice shows or circuses. Both attractions require large casts and usually fill dressing room facilities to the limit; for example, dressing room requirements of a typical major touring ice show are set forth in the show's technical manual:

Enough table space for 44 girls; enough table space for seven principal women; enough table space for 14 boys; enough table space for 9 principal men. In the arenas where we have separate makeup and dressing rooms for the ballet, the requirement for chairs is as follows: 44 chairs in girl's make-up room; 50 chairs in girls dressing room; 14 chairs in boys' makeup room; 20 chairs in boys dressing room. Girls require a minimum of 8 hat tables (banquet type, 8-foot). Boys require a minimum of 3 hat tables.

One room 30′ x 20′ minimum (about 600 square feet) for the principal men. Twenty chairs and dressing tables with 20 mirrors are a necessity. Costume crates go in this room also. (Doors must be at least 30 inches wide to get cases into the rooms).

A room 20' x 20' minimum (about 400 square feet) for the principal girls. Fifteen chairs, 15 mirrors and lights on each table likewise. (Costume crates go into this room, also.)

A room 10' x 10' for the Musical Director, M.C. and staff, road musicians and stagehands. Ten chairs and several mirrors will be sufficient here.

A sewing room 20' x 20' back of the ice area with 2 work tables and 4 chairs.

It should also be noted that dressing rooms must be located in areas in which maximum privacy and protection from the general public can be provided. When possible, athletes and artists should be screened from facility personnel as well. At the same time, dressing rooms must be adjacent to the playing area or stage and within a reasonable distance form an entrance.

For teams and casts of large shows provision should be made to give buses easy access to the stage door or performers' entrance.

OFFICIALS DRESSING ROOMS

League regulations have become substantially more demanding in regard to the location, security, and quality of dressing rooms for game officials.

Primary requirements are for sufficient space to accommodate at least four men (more in the case of stadiums) with showers, toilets, and facilities for hanging clothing. In addition, a good dressing room should contain a small lounge or rest area for the use of officials before games and between periods.

Officials' dressing rooms should have easy access to the playing area; they must be easily screened and protected and should be separated from team dressing rooms.

THEATERS AND PLAYHOUSES

Dressing rooms in theaters and concert halls can be given a substantially more elegant appearance than those in sports-oriented facilities.

Here, again, requirements will depend largely on the type of activity for which the theater has been designed. Those catering primarily to music, for example, may require greater space and attention directed to orchestra and chorus dressing rooms, storage cabinets, conductors rooms, and similar features. The relation between these dressing rooms and the corridors leading to the stage are of great importance to the smooth operation of a theater.

Plans should be carefully discussed and developed with experienced theater consultants. Some consultants recommend a minimum of 50 square feet per person as a design criterion for theatrical and music hall dressing rooms. No attempt is intended here to program dressing rooms for a facility. Rather, we stress the importance of such spaces and the need for careful research of specific requirements.

The Green Room

Common to theaters is the "green room," which is not a dressing room but a place in which actors and musicians can wait for their calls. It is located backstage near the dressing rooms and adjacent to the stage. The "green room" may be looked on as the actors' club room in which they may meet and entertain their friends after a performance. It is here also that meetings between director and cast members may occur.

18. First Aid Rooms

Although often overlooked in planning, properly located and adequately equipped first aid stations may at times be more important than restrooms or perhaps any support feature of a public assembly facility. Many lives have been saved and countless injuries reduced because proper care has been readily available.

The registered nurses, paramedics, Red Cross workers, and other personnel who staff first aid rooms in major facilities may be called on to handle any type of problem ranging from heart attacks and overdoses of drugs to headaches. No longer should a public address announcer have to ask hopefully "Is there a doctor in the house?"

First aid requirements are two or perhaps threefold in nature:

• Proper care must be provided for athletes if it is a sports facility.

- Assistance to the general public is necessary at virtually all gatherings of any size.
- Supplies and at least basic first aid equipment should be readily available for employees and others in the building during non-event times.

SPORTS NEEDS

Turning first to the needs of sports, this emergency facility and its equipment can range anywhere from a simple examination table to a room in which a physician can suture the cuts sustained by professional hockey players. The volume of activity and level of professionalism will dictate the extent of the space and equipment needed.

Supplementing the first aid room in most facilities housing professional or university sports teams are therapy rooms and equipment designed to assist in the treatment of sprains, deep bruises, and muscle pulls. Space for the trainer and his equipment should also be provided.

PUBLIC FIRST AID NEEDS

A public emergency room from which the nurse can move quickly to any part of the building should be centrally located and easily found by the general public. At the same time, its location should be such that when necessary patients can be transported to a hospital or elsewhere in the most expeditious and inconspicuous manner possible. Stretcher cases should be moved to a back or side door accessible to an ambulance.

The sizes of first aid rooms will depend on the capacity of the facility and the number of rooms programmed.

Typically, the emergency room of a large facility will have space for at least two examination tables or hospital beds. (Tables are preferred because of their height, lack of the need for linens, and the fact that patients are seldom retained for any length of time.)

Sliding curtains to give privacy to each table or bed are essential. Other basic equipment includes a nurse's or attendant's station, side chairs, a medicine cabinet, wheelchairs, stretchers, resuscitators, and similar items.

The first aid room should be provided with its own toilet equipped with assistance hardware for the handicapped. Figure 83 shows an example of a well-equipped first aid room.

Lighting should be on dimmers for the convenience of resting patients. Each table or bed, however, will require high-intensity examination lights.

Portable equipment is frequently used in temporary situations. It may be

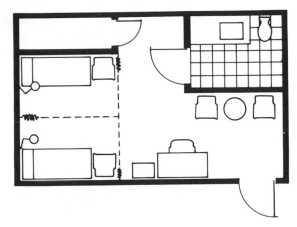

Figure 83. *First Aid Rooms.* A well-designed first aid room for the average-sized arena, exhibition hall, or theater functions as a site for patient care and a base for a nurse or first aid attendent. This sketch shows the nurse's desk and storage cabinet, two beds or examination tables, examination lamps, side chairs, and movable curtains for privacy. Two additional chairs in the reception area, a rest room, and storage closet-complete the arrangement.

necessary to establish a short-term first aid room in an exhibition hall or another area of the building that may be a substantial distance from the permanent station.

One final note. Individual heating and/or cooling of the first aid room should be effected. Its temperature may be detrimental to the welfare of the patient and the attendant may be unable to remedy the situation because of some type of master control.

19. Private Suites

Dubbed "sky boxes" soon after their introduction, private suites quickly became a highly controversial subject in the arena and stadium industry. Representing millions of dollars in construction costs and more millions in potential income, opposition ranged from the propriety of such structures in publicly owned buildings, to esthetics, to the sharing of revenue with touring attractions.

Private suites were first seen in Houston's Astrodome at the upper levels (See Figure 84). Situated at almost the uppermost deck of the huge stadium, the suites thus earned their early nickname.

Almost without exception suites available in arenas and stadiums are leased on an annual basis. They provide the tenant with plush "living rooms" for entertainment and guaranteed seating on decks or special glassed-in areas overlooking the playing field or floor. Some provide

Figure 84. This photograph of a private suite in the Astrodome in Houston shows the finish and furnishings of one of the rooms. Although the original Astrodome suite owners were given considerable latitude in regard to decor and equipment, later facilities have substantially restricted choice of design.

closed-circuit television for guests who prefer not to leave the comforts of the room and bar.

Income from these special boxes is of such consequence that some owners contend they could not have proceeded with construction without these revenues. Most suites contain a carpeted reception area, bar, restroom, and closed-circuit and broadcast television. Seating is provided for 10 to 21 guests, and special parking privileges are accorded to suite purchasers. Food service, bartenders, and waitresses are available at extra cost. In some instances lessees are required to purchase their liquor from the building or its concessionaire. In others, the owner is provided a lockable cabinet in which to store his supply.

Annual rental fees are understandably high. By price tag and concept the private suite personifies superservice. It affords many privileges and conveniences not otherwise obtainable by the ordinary patron. Overwhelmingly patronized by corporations, the "sky box" is charged off as an entertainment expenditure.

At Madison Square Garden in New York, for example, the original annual rental fee for a suite was $50,000. Thus 20 luxury suites brought a handsome revenue each year to the Garden Corporation.

Purchase of tickets to individual events in a facility throughout the year is another matter. In almost all cases the box owner is permitted first refusal on tickets for all events. In some situations he is required to purchase tickets for all—or a specified percentage—of the scheduled activities.

Promoters of events in arenas and stadiums in which private suites are located have contended that they should be entitled to a share of the revenue from the sale of tickets to their shows. Some facility owners have responded that without this income the building rent would necessarily be much higher and therefore the promoter is not entitled to any portion of the income from the sale of tickets.

In spite of their cost, reaction to the availability of the suites in most cities has been good. Management of facilities offering accommodations report a waiting list for boxes. Some point out that a tightening of tax laws could possibly alter the situation but doubt that it would affect their income to any great extent.

From an architectural standpoint private suites have presented design challenges, particularly when they were added after completion of the facility. A few of the problems have been adequate access, compatibility with the balance of the facility, interior lighting without creating glare in the arena, and heating and ventilation.

One stadium manager points out that the concept of executive boxes is far from new. He traces the idea back to the ancient Romans and their coliseums:

It's a throwback to the caste system of those days when the idle rich, who insisted on social status, had individual boxes constructed. They were furnished with all the luxuries associated with those days and the elite used them to separate themselves from the poorer classes.

Still another type of "executive" box is commonplace in European arenas and stadiums in which almost without exception special accommodations are provided for royalty or high governmental officials.

In the United States the presence of special boxes undoubtedly originated in privately owned arenas and stadiums for the use of owners of professional team franchises and their guests. Such facilities have been common to the industry for many years.

Private suites were perhaps a logical step beyond the private clubs commonly found in many arenas and stadiums catering to professional sports. The club concept customarily offers bar service and private dining facilities in a location overlooking or close to the arena or playing field. Club membership is normally limited to season ticket holders who pay additional fees for club privileges.

In most cases the club member receives special parking allocation and, when possible, a special entrance or elevàtor is made available.

20. Public Skating

In many communities, particularly smaller ones, it is not uncommon for arenas to add public skating to their schedules. Special planning should be given to the facilities needed to cater to this activity efficiently and economically.

Because ice skating is primarily a participant sport, the requirements for spectator seating are minimal. As a result many arena operators have provided a special entrance for skaters that gives them direct access to the rink. This move eliminates the use of the main lobby and may discourage loitering in the seating areas.

Arrangements must be made for a ticket window or box office at some point to establish admissions control. After payment of an entry fee, skaters should be able to move freely to a changing area, skate shop, restrooms, concession stands, and the rink itself.

Most skaters can be expected to have their own skates but will require a "changing area" equipped with benches or chairs, rubber matting for safety and coat racks or lockers. Protective floor covering will be required for all areas the skaters may use, including the restrooms.

The skate shop provides rental skates for those who want them. It may also offer a variety of skating wares plus services such as blade sharpening. The layout of the shop may vary but will usually consist of a counter plus racks for the rental skates and a display of items of merchandise for sale.

Location of the skaters entrance, skate shop, restrooms, and other features may also dictate the need for the specification of a special gate or gates in the hockey dashers.

A fast-food stand is a necessary element in a successful skating operation. It should be near the ice and within admissions control. Benches or chairs on which skaters may rest while enjoying their food and drink are also recommended.

Operational economies usually dictate that facility personnel perform a variety of roles during a skating session, making the location of the ticket windows in relation to the skate shop and to the rink of strong importance.

Some degree of arena lighting control should be located near the skate shop or at least in the vicinity of the public skating area. Further, because recorded or taped music and frequent announcements are normally a part of all public skating sessions, controls for operating the public address system should be readily accessible in or near the skate shop.

21. Rates and Policies

Under ideal circumstances, a public assembly facility should serve all community needs, yield sufficient revenue to meet its fixed cost such as debt amortization and interest, pay operating costs, and perhaps even provide a surplus for future maintenance.

Few, if any, facilities have experienced such happy circumstances, thus forcing their government owners or administrative bodies to determine what the financial policies should be.

Many years ago F.G.H Symons reported in a Public Administration Services publication, *Municipal Auditoriums*, that a survey of buildings seemed to indicate that cities had built their facilities with one of three objectives in mind:

- Some had determined that the buildings should be sources of income.
- Some felt the auditoriums should meet their own operating expenses.

• The majority believed that their buildings would always require subsidization from general funds.

The situation has changed little over the years, with the possible exception that under current economic conditions only extreme optimism would permit a government official to see a performing arts center, music hall, or convention center as a source of direct income for his community. It is recognized, however, that the phenomenal popularity of rock music concerts in arenas and stadiums has helped substantially to improve the financial position of those facilities in which such events take place.

With more than 79% of all professional sports facilities and well over that percentage of other audience support facilities under public ownership, the question why local governments should be in the property rental business at all may be valid.

In simplest terms it probably amounts to the fact that if cities, states, and provinces did not provide theaters, arenas, convention halls, and stadiums most of them would probably never be built. The intangible economic and social benefits to the communities in which such facilities are located are usually extensive and citizens are often content to support them. Their worth, however, is difficult to assess in monetary terms, thus placing a highly subjective value on the external benefits derived.

A comprehensive study entitled *"Government and the Sports Business"* was published in 1974 by the Brookings Institution in Washington, D.C. In a chapter on "Subsidies of Stadiums and Arenas," Benjamin A. Okner concludes his report with the following paragraph:

In summary: (1) the rentals charged for use of publicly owned sports facilities vary considerably and any rationale for actual practices followed is difficult to discern; (2) in general, the benefits from publicly owned sports facilities probably accrue disproportionately to the moderate-income or well-to-do citizens in the community at the expense of the poor; and (3) to the extent that subsidized rentals are not passed on to consumers in the form of lower prices or to players in the form of higher salaries, the prime beneficiaries of the local government subsidies are the owners of sports teams—most of whom are extremely wealthy.

Nevertheless, in addition to the pleasure its citizens may derive from cultural attractions, stage presentations, sports events, and shows, a city must also consider the employment provided by the facilities, the spending of convention delegates, increased tax receipts, and possibly even higher incremental taxes from properties located nearby. Such socioeconomic benefits can usually be expanded by those desiring to justify subsidization of a given facility.

As a result, the determination of the proper rates and policies for any publicly owned facility becomes more a matter of identifying purposes and objectives rather than economics; for example, if the stadium rent is so high that a professional sports tenant decides not to play in that facility, the entire purpose of the project may be lost. The same theory is applicable to convention halls, performing arts centers, and arenas.

Again quoting Okner:

Probably the most practical suggestion is that in studying a given stadium operation, consideration always should be given to whether the direct financial losses might be offset somewhat or balanced by the presence of net intangible benefits.

Generally speaking, because of their adaptability and multiplicity of purpose, arenas exhibit better opportunities to recover at least operating costs than do theaters and concert halls. Even so, management will quickly discover that rental rates must be comparable to those of other facilities of similar size and location if they wish to attract the desired shows and events.

Promoters scheduling and routing shows across the nation are well aware of acceptable rental terms and resist dealing with buildings that may prove more expensive—especially if nothing extra is included for the difference or if alternative facilities are available in that particular market.

As a rule, it can be noted that most arenas operate under a minimum rental fee or a percentage of the gross gate receipts, whichever is the greater. The practice is generally the same for stadiums. Many offer "ceilings" or maximum rent figures for certain high-grossing shows.

Theaters, however, because of their limited seating capacity, are normally limited to making a flat rental charge, with some variation possible based on the type of event.

Some of the criteria that may enter into consideration when rental fees are established are the following:

- Basic rates
- Extra equipment or services
- Commercial versus nonprofit users
- Paid or free admission
- Type of activity
- Matinee and/or evening performances
- Charges on a percentage basis
- Duration of occupancy
- Rehearsal/practice time
- Resident versus nonresident users
- Seasonal variations
- Concessions income
- Parking income

BASIC RATES

Basic rates may depend on a variety of factors. Although computation of the anticipated variable operating costs divided by the anticipated number of rentals or uses would perhaps serve as an idealistic starting point, the figure that would result might well leave the facility standing idle to a point of embarrassment for both owner and management. Most facilities appear to have adopted rental fees commensurate with those found in like facilities located in similar-sized communities. Under analysis this process may be worthy of consideration if the building is to be of strong interest to potential users.

EXTRA EQUIPMENT OR SERVICES

Many facilities have found that by making a capital investment in certain equipment it is possible to develop additional revenue from its rental or possibly by increasing the basic rate to include its cost.

Many buildings often provide services such as admissions control, ticket handling, and security. Additional charges are made to recover the cost of this labor.

COMMERCIAL VERSUS NONPROFIT USERS

It may be desirable to consider lowering rents for conventions and other strictly noncommercial users. The rental structure however, must be written to prevent commercial users from leasing the facilities under the name or auspices of noncommercial or nonprofit groups to circumvent the intent.

Many cities have adopted special rates for conventions and religious, educational, or charitable organizations. The use is confined to bonafide meetings or functions of these groups.

As a definition of terms, some facilities classify religious, educational, and charitable organizations as

those whose funds go totally to non-profit, tax-free institutions; that no salaries for talent may be paid performers or members of the institutions except to executive personnel, i.e., scoutmasters, ministers; and, further, that any proceeds from the sale of advertising in programs and sale of same shall go to the non-profit, tax-free institution in its entirety.

PAID OR FREE ADMISSION

Rental rates seldom vary between paid or free admissions when special terms are in effect for nonprofit organizations.

OVERTIME

Overtime charges are normally made a part of rental fee structures to prohibit lengthy meetings or events beyond the normal shifts of facility personnel. Inclusion of this ruling in contract terms helps to enforce building regulations.

INGRESS/EGRESS

Ingress/egress (move-in/move-out) charges have a high degree of variance, depending on the demand for the facility. Perhaps the most common rental fee is one-half the amount of the regular daily rate. Most facilities, however, provide some in-and-out time without charge; the subject is normally a matter of negotiation, depending on the conditions.

DURATION OF OCCUPANCY

Because only limited economies may accrue to the facility as a result of multiple-date use, there is little reason to offer discounts. Few facilities do so.

REHEARSALS OR PRACTICE TIME

As with ingress/egress, charges for rehearsals or practice time have a high variance that depends on facility demand. In order to present a given attraction, some rehearsal or practice time may be mandatory. Depending on how this time affects accommodation of the needs of other uses by the facility rehearsal/practice time rates of about one-half the basic rate are normally in effect.

SEASONAL VARIATIONS

Seasonal variations in the basic rate are not uncommon as an enticement to bring events into a building during the summer months or in what may be termed marginal periods by the promoter or event producer.

CONCESSIONS/PARKING INCOME

Lease negotiations with professional sports teams and others may often bring the facility's income from concessions or parking into discussion. Lessees are quick to point out that it is their activities that attract the spectators who purchase concessions items and leave their cars in the arena or stadium parking lot. Facility owners counter that retention of this income enables them to maintain basic rental rates at the lowest possible level.

ESTABLISHMENT OF RENTAL RATES

The method by which rental rates and policies are established and a system for their change have been found to be important in determining the fiscal success or failure of a public assembly facility.

Whenever possible, fees should be established by knowledgeable administrators who will work closely with experienced managers or consultants. Adjustment of rates may be necessary soon after opening a facility if variable expenses appear to be far in excess of those anticipated or if the established rental figures are creating hardships on potential users of the building.

When legislation authorizing or creating facilities provides for rental rates and policies to be established by ordinance, political considerations have often delayed a necessary increase in rental fees for long periods of time. Such procrastination has brought undesirable financial results and often unfavorable public opinion of the facility and its management.

Ideally, rental rates should be economic rather than political matters.

22. Rules and Regulations

Reflecting government jurisdiction, administrative bodies, local ordinances, and myriad other factors, rules and regulations applying to the use of public assembly facilities can be expected to exhibit a considerable degree of variance.

Recent years, however, have seen the gradual development of more comprehensive contract terms and operating conditions. Some of this stabilization may be attributed to shows and artists who travel extensively and their need for reasonable standardization. Some of the program may be the result of repeated surveys and studies conducted by the International Association of Auditorium Managers.

Regardless of origin, here are some of the subjects that may appear among the standard rules and regulations of a typical facility and are usually part of all lease agreements, permits, or contracts. The many exceptions to each of these items should be noted, however, particularly in long-term agreements or leases with professional sports teams.

LEASE AGREEMENTS

All agreements covering the leasing of space, use of facilities, or provision of services are normally in writing and are signed by all parties concerned.

REGULAR SERVICES

Contracts stipulate services that are included in rental fees: heating (sometimes air conditioning), house lighting, ventilation, regular house cleaning before and after the event, dressing rooms and setups; for example, a basketball court, folding chairs, portable stage.

INCIDENTAL SERVICES

Contracts usually state that services in addition to those regularly supplied shall be furnished only as requested and agreed to by facility management. The tenant, however, is charged for all special or additional services and labor.

PAYMENTS

Contracts customarily stipulate the amount of deposit required, if any, and the method by which the balance due shall be paid.

CONCESSIONS AND CATERING

Because concessions rights are leased on an exclusive basis, most contracts stipulate this fact and point out that the lessee will not participate in any receipts therefrom. In many facilities the same situation prevails for catering.

FIRE

Contracts stipulate that in the event a facility is destroyed or damaged by fire or by any other means that will prevent fulfillment of the contract, the facility is not responsible to the lessee for termination of the rental permit.

CONTROL OF BUILDING

A "control-of-building" clause should point out that in making space available to the lessee the facility is *not* relinquishing the right to control the management of it and to enforce all the necessary and proper rules. Further, it is usually specified that management and its employees may enter the leased premises at any time.

BOX OFFICE FACILITIES AND ADMISSIONS CONTROL

Because most facilities have established relations with ticket-handling organizations and/or unions for admissions control, restrictions on this aspect of a lessee's operations are usually set forth in all contracts.

EXHIBITORS

Primarily applicable to exhibition halls catering to trade shows and conventions, some portion of all contracts ordinarily sets forth the hall's right to remove an exhibitor's display from the building if the exhibitor fails to move it within the stipulated time. The facility also states that it may charge for such service and/or assess an additional charge to the lessee for overtime use of the display space.

ELECTRICITY

Many exhibition halls levy additional charges for the electric energy consumed by exhibitors during trade and consumer shows. This fact, and regulations concerning the right to make electric hookups, is customarily set forth in detail.

WATER

Most exhibition halls provide water only for ordinary drinking, toilet, or janitorial purposes. Additional water for other purposes may elicit an extra charge under some circumstances. The facility policy is customarily spelled out in rules and regulations.

LAW OBSERVANCE

Almost without exception attorneys for public facilities recommend a paragraph in all regulations which states that everyone involved in the event or function must "abide by, conform to and comply with" all rules and regulations for controlling the building and with all rules and regulations of the police and fire department.

SEATING CAPACITY

Lessees are normally prohibited in writing from selling tickets in excess of the established seating capacity of the space leased.

DEFACEMENT OF BUILDING

For public assembly facilities defacement of property is a vital part of the regulations and contract. Lessees are adjured not to drive any "nails, hooks, tacks or screws" into any part of the building nor to make any alterations to the building—including painting. Further, this section of the rules usually points out that the lessee shall also be responsible for the acts of his employees or patrons.

When extraordinary risk of damage is anticipated, the lessee may be required to post a cash deposit in a substantial amount to ensure his cooperation in protecting the property and in making certain that funds are readily available for any necessary repairs.

ASSIGNMENTS

Most facilities prohibit subletting of a contract or use of the building for a purpose other than specified. The reason, of course, is to prevent leasing the facility for one event and discovering later that the lessee had quite a different activity in mind—one that might even be illegal or considered undesirable in the community.

RESPONSIBILITY FOR PROPERTY

A common stipulation is the facility's disclaimer of responsibility for any property brought into the building by the lessee or others.

INTERMISSIONS

Because a substantial portion of any arena's income is derived from concessions, the subject of intermissions during an event is important to the building and its concessionaire. To avoid any misunderstandings most facilities require an intermission of some specified time unless the matter is waived beforehand by building management.

INDEMNITY

In these days of high personal injury claims and judgments liability is a vital concern of all facilities. Most building regulations require that the lessee furnish evidence of liability insurance of certain specific limits, in which the facility is named as an additional beneficiary. This helps to reduce the amount of the building's liability insurance premiums.

HANDLING OF FUNDS

Whether or not box office facilities are provided, most regulations stipulate that the facility shall not be responsible for any funds except in the event of gross neglect or bad faith.

FREE SAMPLES

As a protection to the concessionaire and/or caterer, most facilities prohibit distribution of samples—particularly of food and beverages—without approval of management.

RADIO AND TELEVISION RIGHTS

For sports-oriented facilities contracts must deal with the subject of radio, commercial television and closed-circuit or cable television rights. In some cases facilities consider television income as "gate receipts" and demand a percentage of the total.

SIGN AND POSTERS

Entertainment attractions and some types of conventions bring forth many signs and posters. Because they can cause damage to painted walls and also annoy other lessees, most contracts provide that such advertising material be displayed only in the locations provided by the building.

LOST ARTICLES

It is perhaps unusual, but many facilities insist that the building has the sole right to collect and retain custody of lost articles. The main purpose is to establish an orderly lost-and-found department and to prohibit "poachers" from searching through the seating areas after an event is over.

REENTRY BY OWNER

A standard form clause in most contracts provides for the right of the owner to reenter the leased portion of the building in the event of unanticipated vacancy by the lessee.

23. Marketing The Public Assembly Facility

Although still questioned by some as a proper function of government agencies, the marketing of public assembly facilities is fast becoming a familiar activity in most major cities throughout North America.

The proliferation of arenas in many marginal markets coupled with the rapidly increasing number of convention centers has made the boosting of promotional budgets and manpower a virtual necessity.

In many instances the promotion and marketing of a public assembly facility is an economic requirement. The building must have rental income to meet its operating expenses. It follows, therefore, that potential users must be made aware of the facility and its availability.

In other situations in which income is not the prime interest, frequency of use, the socioeconomic benefits of bringing new convention and visitor dollars to the community, and the variety of attractions are often matters of even greater concern.

Whatever the reason, one of the first objectives in the development of a successful sales program is an analysis of the market. Perhaps the first obvious factor is that only a few people or organizations have any need whatsoever to rent an arena, theater, exhibition hall, or perhaps even a meeting room.

ARENAS

If the marketing objective is greater use of an arena, selling starts with individuals who use and need arenas—athletic directors, professional team managers, executives of ice shows and circuses, rock concert promoters, and similar entrepreneurs.

Management must become familiar with the identity of those individuals who make the decisions to use a particular site. The prospective user should know that the facility is available for his type of activity, that the building manager and staff are interested, and that they can be counted on for help if needed.

Facilities should be listed in all available directories such as *AudArena Stadium Guide* and *Talent & Booking Directory*. Most of these listings are free or extremely low in cost.

Display advertising in one or more trade publications has many advocates. Certainly it is vital to establish or reinforce the identity of facilities that are seeking national and regional users.

EXHIBITION HALLS

Seeking potential users of an exhibition hall is a task similar to that of arena sales except that there are more prospects. Here some innovative thinking may be needed to develop lessees if none are readily available.

If a home, boat, sports, trailer, or similar consumer show is not presently operating in a community, the opening of an exposition hall may be the occasion to encourage the creation of such an event. Lacking local promoters, facility management may have to look elsewhere for individuals or firms that are interested in introducing new events.

Smaller existing shows may have growth potential. Many are in need of larger facilities but have been limited by space or some other problem. Encouragement and opportunity may be all that is needed to move the event into larger quarters.

THEATERS/CONCERT HALLS

Theaters and concert halls usually offer a broader base of potential users than arenas. Adding to the regular list of concert promoters, symphony societies, and operatic groups is a wide variety of local users and an even greater assortment of uses.

Reports of good business travels rapidly. Consequently successful results at the box office should be promptly reported to the trade press.

On the local level management can exploit the fact that a facility is available for rent by speaking whenever possible to groups such as service clubs and school organizations. Managers of new buildings will find more than ample opportunity to appear before these groups.

CONVENTION CENTERS

Convention halls and conference centers present a substantially different picture, for almost without exception convention sales require cooperation with convention bureaus, hotel sales directors, and other segments of the community's "visitor industry."

Again, the size of the facility, population of the community, and the amount of the convention sales budget will to a great degree determine the facility manager's involvement in this aspect of the marketing picture.

In smaller communities the manager may be serving in a major role and working directly with the hotel/motel industry by inviting conventions to the city. In larger metropolitan areas in which major hotels with sales personnel are located the facility manager's responsibility may be more that of supporting and assisting the sales activities of the convention bureau.

In either event the facility manager can help his community and the building by analyzing his property to determine exactly what its capabilities may be; for example, the number of exhibit booths that can be accommodated in exhibit areas; the seating capacity of each room under varying conditions, and the number of people that can be served at food functions.

With more than 38,000 association-sponsored conventions and trade shows in the United States, the prequalification of sales "prospects" for a particular facility is a virtual necessity. If an organization needs space for 400 exhibit booths and a facility can accommodate only 200, then time, money and effort may be wasted in bidding for that convention. Conversely, there may be hundreds of groups whose convention requirements coincide with available facilities. It is these that should constitute the primary marketing objectives.

Whether handled by the convention bureau manager, the facility director, or both, once the profile of the "target" market has been determined, a long-range promotional plan will call for the early establishment of an adequate filing and record-keeping system. Prospective associations must be kept informed of details regarding the facility, and the specific needs of each potential client must be noted.

Direct mail campaigns have been helpful. Many experienced managers use letters, coupled with personal contacts and telephone calls, as highly effective sales tools.

Sometimes these personal contacts may be in the form of a sales "blitz" when teams of convention bureau and hotel/motel industry representatives from a given community visit those cities in which numbers of convention association executives are headquartered.

Often an association will require pledges of assistance in one form or another from a member, club, or chapter of its association in the prospective convention city. Sometimes the requirement may be a simple invitation; at other times the providing of a convention chairman. In any event a convention marketing plan can often require more "selling" of the idea locally than on the association level.

Even more than arenas and theaters, convention facilities must be listed in every available directory. A number of trade publications cater to the convention and meetings industry and their availability has made display advertising a major thrust for most of the more active centers. Expenditures for such media campaigns appear to be growing annually as competition increases.

'Finally, there is the process of following up, updating of files, and repeating the process over and over again.

Adding still another dimension to the problem of marketing convention facilities is the cyclical or rotational nature of most association meetings. In other words, an association may meet one year in the eastern part of the United States, the next year in the midwest, the next in the south, and the next in the west. Obviously, then, if a city loses a bid for a particular year, it will probably have to wait three more years before another invitation will even be considered.

Other factors also come into play. Some associations will consider only "sunshine" cities; some want a resort atmosphere, some a "big city"; others want an institutional backdrop and still others want an area in which members may visit factories, institutions, or businesses connected with their particular industry or profession.

All in all, a community must have the features a particular association considers necessary if it expects to win the bid.

Marketers of convention and conference centers cannot overlook the hundreds of industry-oriented or professional meetings conducted annually throughout North America. Although perhaps not officially listed as a convention, such activities still require meeting facilities, hotel rooms, and other support services of the community.

MEETING ROOMS

Finally, most facilities have meeting rooms. Meeting rooms differ from other portions of a complex because the base for potential users is so broad. Potential lessees range from families planning wedding receptions to industrial firms organizing sales meetings.

Many buildings have experienced excellent results with direct mail campaigns among industries and other businesses in the community in which their attention is called to the availability of space. It is, however, a program that must be repeated frequently because of the constant change of personnel in charge of such functions.

Meeting rooms should be listed in the yellow pages of the local telephone directory.

Perhaps the greatest help in developing increased use of meeting rooms is word-of-mouth advertising. When accommodations and service are pleasing, the satisfied lessee is quick to recommend a facility to others. A follow-up plan by management to determine results and attitudes after meeting room events is strongly suggested.

Whether the primary objective is rental revenues or heavy community use, the goal can be attained more quickly by aggressive and intelligent marketing plans. Marketing, however, is not a one-time process. Progress must be reviewed periodically; goals must be reappraised and the entire project started all over again.

24. Community Role of the Facility

The role of a public assembly facility in community development should be one of influence and importance. Events and attractions can make a city a better place in which to live. The very presence and prominence of a well-designed structure can become a symbol of local pride and progress.

Essentially a community resource, an audience support facility can relate to local goals and objectives in many ways. Through its staff and management it should serve as a focal point for many worthwhile developments.

First and foremost a building should be operated to perform its intended function to the best extent possible. Whether conceived for theatrical purposes, conventions, sports, trade shows, or community activities, every effort should be made to ensure that the facility fulfills that objective.

If the purpose of the facility is to attract convention delegate dollars to the community, its management should be active in the convention bureau, the Chamber of Commerce, or whatever group handles marketing responsibilities for conventions and meetings in the city. The manager must be familiar with the convention hotels of his community, and must work with them in developing available date structures and acceptable rental terms.

When a facility caters primarily to entertainment or the performing arts, the manager must be available to and compatible with those in the cultural and arts segment of his community. He must identify with the leaders in the local symphony, ballet, or opera. He must help commercial promoters "find" available dates for attractions that should be seen in his community.

If the facility is essentially for community use, the manager should be professional, patient, and interested in working with amateur groups to help bring many of the locally oriented community activities to reality.

The manager of a sports facility must be interested in introducing a broad range of athletic events into the building. By contacts with local sportswriters and sportscasters he must remind them that their promotional assistance is needed to make local sports offerings successful.

At the same time, it is necessary that residents of the community hold a high regard for the facility and its operation. The deportment of ticket sellers, ticket takers, ushers, door guards, and others is of great concern, for their treatment of and attitude toward the public *are* those of the facility, its management, and ownership. If these "public contact" people are calloused, rude, and careless, there is a good chance that the community will conclude that management and public officials are the same.

Of great importance in establishing the image of a facility is housekeeping. The cleanliness and effciency of the concessions department, for example, is vital. The competency of the maintenance and custodial staff must say, loud and clear—"we care!."

Finally, the facility manager should perform his role in a professional manner. In many cities he may be the only knowledgeable resource to the community in his chosen field.

Through the influence of a successful building a community may be led to the development and construction of additional facilities. If located in the central business district, it could be instrumental in redirecting attention to the core area and in helping to preserve the role of downtown America.

The role of the facility in community development cannot be underestimated—and especially so under intelligent, well-directed management.

25. Administration

Development of the proper administrative system for a public assembly facility has long been a matter of debate and conjecture. Some elaborate programs to ensure sound management policies have failed. Conversely, many simple arrangements have proved to be extremely successful.

Many variations can be found, but four basic administrative plans appear to prevail.

Civic Department

The facility becomes a "department" or branch of a city, county, state, or provincial organization in which the manager is directly responsible to the city manager, county executive, mayor, or similar official.

187

Branch of a Civic Department

The facility is operated by a manager who reports to a civic department head such as parks and recreation director or public works director. Operation is much the same as an independent civic department except that such arrangements do not usually accord the facility the same status and identity as they would a separate department.

Independent Authority

The facility is governed by an independent board of directors, commission, authority, or similar body appointed by the mayor, governor, or other elected official. In some cases such boards are advisory. Some are fiscally independent; others are subject to budget approval from elected officials.

Private Operation

Management and operation is provided by a private corporation or organization under a lease or contract providing for a specified fee or compensation. In the case of private ownership administration is provided by the owner or a board of directors representing the stockholders.

Direct control of publicly owned buildings and complexes by individual departments prevails throughout North America as the most common form of administration. A survey of more than 300 facilities in 1974 revealed that slightly more than 50% of the managers responding reported directly to a city manager, mayor, or the head of some city or county department.

Approximately 30% of the reporting facilities in the International Association of Auditorium Managers survey indicated that they were under the administrative guidance of a "building board," board of control, board of directors, or some similar body. All such bodies have varying degrees of authority and autonomy, ranging from power to assess and collect tax revenues to the mere advising of the manager on policy matters.

In university and college-owned facilities management almost without exception is responsible directly to the president or the chancellor's office.

Much can be said in favor of an autonomous or independent authority. Such bodies are ostensibly free from political influence. The facility may be permitted to set itself apart from certain municipal employee commitments and labor agreements of the government jurisdiction; purchasing procedures are normally less restrictive, and the authority can establish operational practices common to the private sector.

Such an administrative authority can prove valuable to political bodies as well by providing them with "insulation" from pressures in contract negotiations, preferential rental dates, jobs, and other matters. When an autonomous body has been permitted to remain so, some excellent results have been recorded.

The fact remains, however, that seldom can an independent body permanently remain outside the political arena. Its members are usually appointed by some political figure, and often such appointments carry with them a commitment to accomplish certain objectives.

Statutes and ordinances that establish independent boards or advisory committees require city, county, or state approval of budgets and/or operating expenses. Subtle—or sometimes not so subtle—pressures can easily be applied by such fiscal controls.

Political theorists are quick to note that autonomous boards are not truly "democratic," for their members are usually not elected by the citizenry and therefore cannot be removed from office except by formal charges or perhaps by the request of the appointing official.

Inherent with creation of autonomous or advisory bodies is the constant problem of finding knowledgeable persons to serve. Normally there is no compensation and often there is public criticism. In most cases a new appointee is unfamiliar with the entertainment, convention, or sports industry and must undergo considerable indoctrination before being truly prepared to evaluate many of the issues on which he is asked to rule.

Recent years have seen an increase in the number of facilities in which the manager is a department head in city government responsible directly to the city manager. From many standpoints this system provides for a more direct organizational plan and has much to recommend its adoption.

Most projects are paid for with public funds and require continuing financial support from special taxes or the general fund. As a community resource, a facility should not be set apart from other city functions, for it generally requires considerable assistance from other departments in order to realize its total capabilities.

Ideally, an administrative plan would provide a manager with a board of experienced directors capable of assisting him in making policy decisions in all areas of responsibility. It would be a body free from political, business, or labor pressures. The board members would not be appointed specifically to represent special interest groups but rather to assist in administering the facility in the most intelligent and equitable fashion possible.

Until such a Utopian goal can be achieved, existing systems—or variations thereof—are probably the best of today's options.

Architectural Credits

Madison Square Garden, Charles Luckman & Associates
The Forum (Los Angeles), Charles Luckman & Associates
Los Angeles Center, Welton Becket & Associates
Lincoln Center:

   Vivian Beaumont Theater, Eero Saarinen & Associates
   New York State Theater, Philip Johnson
   Metropolitan Opera House, Harrison & Abramovitz
   Avery Fisher Hall, Johnson & Burgee

Grady Gammage Theater, Frank Lloyd Wright
Oakland Coliseum Complex, Skidmore, Owings & Merrill
Louisiana Superdome, Curtis & Davis and Associates
Astrodome, Lloyd & Morgan; Wilson, Morris, Crain & Anderson
Kingdome, Naramore, Skillings & Praeger
Las Vegas Convention Center, Adrian Wilson & Associates

San Antonio Convention Center, Thomas Noonan & Associates
Los Angeles Coliseum, John and Donald B. Parkinson
McCormick Place, C. F. Murphy Associates
University of Illinois Assembly Hall, Harrison & Abramovitz
Spokane Riverpark Theater, Walker, McGough, Lyerla & Foltz

Editorial Acknowledgments

American Institute of Architects
American Seating Company
AudArena Stadium Guide, a Billboard Publication
William A. Cunningham, Oakland-Alameda County Coliseum Complex
International Association of Auditorium Managers
International Association of Convention and Visitor Bureaus
Thomas F. Liegler, Anaheim Convention Center/Stadium
Thomas D. Minter, Lexington Center Corporation
John H. Poelker, Mayor, City of St. Louis
Roy G. Saunders, Tulsa Public Events Department

Index